# Knocking on Democracy's Door

Bradley Hall

Published by Bradley Hall, 2024.

KNOCKING ON DEMOCRACY'S DOOR

**First edition. September 5, 2024.**



ISBN: 979-8338454473

Written by Bradley Hall.

# Table of Contents

# Chapter 1: Introduction to Doorknocking

## Overview of Doorknocking as a Powerful Grassroots Campaign Tool

In the digital age, where campaigns often rely heavily on social media, email, and targeted online ads, it's easy to underestimate the power of traditional, face-to-face interaction. Yet, doorknocking, a method that has been a staple of grassroots political campaigns for decades, remains one of the most effective tools in a campaign's arsenal. The essence of doorknocking is simple: going door-to-door in a community to speak directly with voters, share information about a candidate or issue, and gather support. Despite its simplicity, doorknocking is a complex and highly strategic endeavor that can significantly influence election outcomes.

The power of doorknocking lies in its personal touch. Unlike a television ad or a social media post, a face-to-face conversation allows for genuine human connection. When you knock on a voter's door, you are not just a campaign volunteer; you are a representative of the candidate or cause. This personal interaction can make a voter feel valued and heard, which is something that digital interactions often fail to achieve. The ability to engage directly with voters, answer their questions, address their concerns, and understand their needs is unparalleled in other forms of campaigning.

Doorknocking is also a versatile tool that can be adapted to various campaign needs. Whether you're trying to introduce a relatively unknown candidate, persuade undecided voters, or ensure that supporters turn out to vote, doorknocking allows you to tailor your approach to specific goals. For example, in the early stages of a campaign, doorknocking might focus on raising awareness and educating voters about a candidate's platform. As the election approaches, the focus might shift to mobilizing supporters and getting out the vote.

Furthermore, doorknocking provides campaigns with valuable data that can inform broader strategy. Every interaction at the doorstep offers insights into voter sentiment, preferences, and priorities. This information can be used to refine campaign messages, target specific voter segments, and allocate resources more effectively. In many ways, doorknocking serves as both a direct outreach method and a feedback mechanism, helping campaigns stay responsive to the electorate.

## Importance of Personal Interaction in Political Campaigns

Personal interaction has always been a cornerstone of political campaigning, but its importance has only grown in an era where voters are bombarded with information from countless sources. In such a saturated environment, personal interaction stands out as a meaningful and memorable experience. It cuts through the noise, allowing a campaign to connect with voters on a deeper level.

One of the key benefits of personal interaction is the ability to build trust. Trust is a critical factor in how people make decisions, especially when it comes to voting. A voter is more likely to support a candidate if they feel that the candidate genuinely cares about their concerns and is committed to representing their interests. When a campaign volunteer takes the time to knock on someone's door, it signals that the campaign values that voter's opinion. This gesture can go a long way in building the trust needed to win votes.

Personal interaction also allows for nuanced communication that is difficult to achieve through other means. Campaign messages delivered via television or social media are often broad and generalized, designed to appeal to a wide audience. In contrast, a face-to-face conversation at the doorstep can be highly personalized. Volunteers can tailor their message based on the specific concerns and interests of the voter. For instance, if a voter is particularly concerned about healthcare, the volunteer can focus on the candidate's healthcare policies. This level of personalization can make the campaign message more relevant and compelling to the voter.

Moreover, personal interaction is a two-way street. While the campaign volunteer is there to share information, they also have the opportunity to listen. Listening is a powerful tool in building rapport and trust. When voters feel that their concerns are being heard and taken seriously, they are more likely to engage with the campaign and consider its message. This dynamic is particularly important in areas where voters may feel neglected or disenfranchised. By showing up at their door and listening to their concerns, a campaign can demonstrate that it values every vote and every voice.

Personal interaction through doorknocking also helps humanize the candidate. In an age of media saturation, candidates can often appear distant and out of touch with the everyday lives of voters. Doorknocking bridges this gap by putting a face to the campaign. Voters are more likely to support a candidate who they perceive as approachable, empathetic, and connected to their community. When volunteers engage with voters, they can share stories and insights that highlight the candidate's character, values, and commitment to the community, making the candidate more relatable and trustworthy.

## The Impact of Doorknocking on Voter Turnout and Election Results

The effectiveness of doorknocking in increasing voter turnout and influencing election results is well-documented. Numerous studies and analyses have shown that direct voter contact, particularly through doorknocking, is one of the most effective ways to mobilize voters. This impact is particularly pronounced in close races, where every vote counts.

One of the primary reasons doorknocking is so effective at boosting voter turnout is its ability to cut through voter apathy. In many elections, a significant portion of the electorate may be undecided or indifferent. They might not feel strongly about any particular candidate or issue, or they may feel that their vote doesn't matter. Doorknocking addresses this apathy by providing voters with a tangible reminder of the election and an opportunity to engage directly with the campaign. A face-to-face conversation can motivate a voter to participate in the election, especially if they feel that the campaign has taken the time to reach out to them personally.

In addition to increasing voter turnout, doorknocking can also have a significant impact on how people vote. Persuasion is a key component of doorknocking, particularly when targeting undecided voters or those who may lean toward an opposing candidate. A well-executed doorknocking campaign can change minds by addressing voters' concerns, providing new information, and making a compelling case for the candidate. This persuasive power is particularly important in swing districts or states, where a small shift in voter preference can change the outcome of an election.

The data gathered during doorknocking campaigns also plays a crucial role in shaping broader campaign strategy. By tracking voter interactions and responses, campaigns can identify trends, assess the effectiveness of their messaging, and make data-driven decisions about where to focus their efforts. For example, if a particular issue resonates strongly with voters in a specific area, the campaign can adjust its messaging to emphasize that issue more heavily in future outreach efforts. This targeted approach not only maximizes the impact of the campaign but also ensures that resources are allocated efficiently.

In some cases, the impact of doorknocking can be the difference between winning and losing an election. In close races, where the margin of victory is often razor-thin, the votes gained through doorknocking can be decisive. This is particularly true in down-ballot races, where voter awareness and engagement are often lower, and where a personal touch can make a significant difference.

**Setting Expectations: What You Will Encounter**

Doorknocking is an incredibly rewarding activity, but it is not without its challenges. Setting realistic expectations is crucial for anyone who plans to engage in doorknocking as part of a political campaign. Understanding what you might encounter will help you prepare mentally and emotionally, ensuring that you can stay motivated and effective throughout the campaign.

One of the first things to understand is that not every interaction will be positive. While many voters will appreciate the effort you are making, others may be indifferent, and some may be openly hostile. It's important to approach each door with an open mind and a thick skin. Not everyone will agree with your candidate or cause, and some people may express their disagreement in ways that are less than polite. It's crucial to remember that you are representing your campaign and to maintain a calm and respectful demeanor, even in the face of negativity.

You should also be prepared for a variety of logistical challenges. Doorknocking involves a significant amount of physical activity, including walking long distances, standing for extended periods, and sometimes dealing with harsh weather conditions. Proper preparation is key to staying comfortable and safe. Wearing comfortable shoes, dressing appropriately for the weather, and staying hydrated are all essential. Additionally, you should be prepared for the possibility of encountering obstacles such as gated communities, locked apartment buildings, or homes with "No Soliciting" signs. In these cases, it's important to know your campaign's guidelines on how to proceed or when to move on to the next location.

Another aspect of doorknocking that requires preparation is managing your time effectively. Depending on the size of the area you are covering and the number of homes you plan to visit, doorknocking can be a time-consuming process. It's important to balance the quality of your interactions with the quantity of doors you knock on. While it's valuable to spend time engaging in meaningful conversations with voters, you also need to ensure that you are reaching as many voters as possible. This may involve making quick judgments about when to continue a conversation and when to move on to the next door.

In addition to these practical challenges, doorknocking also presents emotional challenges. Campaigning can be an emotional rollercoaster, with moments of exhilaration and moments of frustration. You may encounter voters who share moving personal stories or express deep gratitude for your work, which can be incredibly rewarding. On the other hand, you may also encounter voters who express anger, disillusionment, or apathy, which can be disheartening. It's important to stay focused on your mission and to remember that every door you knock on is an opportunity to make a difference, even if it doesn't feel that way in the moment.

Finally, it's important to set realistic expectations about the impact of your efforts. While doorknocking is a powerful tool, it is just one part of a larger campaign strategy. Not every voter you speak with will be persuaded, and not every door you knock on will result in a conversation. However, every interaction contributes to the overall success of the campaign, whether by raising awareness, gathering data, or simply showing that the campaign cares enough to engage directly with voters.

Doorknocking is a challenging but highly rewarding activity that can have a significant impact on a political campaign. By understanding the power of personal interaction, recognizing the impact doorknocking can have on voter turnout and election results, and setting realistic expectations for what you will encounter, you can approach doorknocking with the confidence and resilience needed to make a difference. Whether you're a seasoned campaigner or a first-time volunteer, the skills and experiences you gain from doorknocking will serve you well, both in this campaign and in future endeavors.

# Chapter 2: Understanding Your Mission

**Defining Your Goals: What Are You Trying to Achieve?**

Before you set out to knock on doors and engage with voters, it's crucial to have a clear understanding of your mission. What are you trying to achieve? In the context of a political campaign, the answer might seem straightforward: to help your candidate win. But the path to that victory is nuanced and multi-faceted. It involves a series of smaller, specific goals that contribute to the broader objective. Understanding these goals will not only make your doorknocking efforts more effective but will also give you a sense of purpose and direction as you engage with voters.

At its core, your mission as a doorknocker is to build support for your candidate or cause. This support can manifest in various ways: persuading undecided voters, solidifying the commitment of existing supporters, encouraging voter turnout, and even gathering valuable data that can inform the campaign's broader strategy. Each interaction you have at the doorstep is an opportunity to move the needle in one of these areas.

**1. Persuasion**

One of the primary goals of doorknocking is persuasion—convincing undecided voters to support your candidate. In many campaigns, a significant portion of the electorate remains undecided until the final weeks, or even days, before an election. These voters often represent the critical swing votes that can determine the outcome of a close race. Your mission, therefore, is to engage these voters in meaningful conversations, address their concerns, and present a compelling case for why your candidate deserves their vote.

Persuasion is not about delivering a monologue or overwhelming voters with information. It's about understanding their priorities, addressing their doubts, and demonstrating that your candidate aligns with their values and interests. This requires a nuanced approach, as each voter may have different concerns or motivations. By listening carefully and responding thoughtfully, you can build trust and influence their decision-making process.

## 2. Voter Identification and Support Solidification

Another key goal is identifying supporters and solidifying their commitment to your candidate. Voter identification involves distinguishing between strong supporters, leaners (those who are inclined to support your candidate but are not fully committed), undecided voters, and those who oppose your candidate. This information is invaluable to the campaign, as it helps prioritize follow-up efforts, especially in the final push before election day.

For strong supporters, your mission is to ensure that they remain engaged and committed. This might involve reminding them of the importance of voting, offering them volunteer opportunities, or simply reinforcing their enthusiasm for the candidate. For leaners, your goal is to address any lingering doubts or concerns they may have, helping to turn their inclination into a firm commitment.

## 3. Voter Mobilization

Voter mobilization is a critical aspect of any campaign, and doorknocking plays a significant role in this effort. Even if a voter is fully committed to supporting your candidate, their vote only counts if they actually show up at the polls. Your mission includes encouraging and reminding voters to participate in the election, particularly in areas where voter turnout may be historically low.

This can involve providing information about polling locations, voting hours, and absentee or early voting options. In some cases, you might also identify and address potential barriers to voting, such as lack of transportation or confusion about voting procedures. Ensuring that supporters are informed, prepared, and motivated to vote is a crucial part of your mission.

## 4. Data Collection and Feedback

Every conversation you have at the doorstep provides valuable data that can inform the campaign's broader strategy. This data might include information about voter preferences, concerns, and priorities, as well as insights into the effectiveness of the campaign's messaging. By collecting and reporting this information, you help the campaign refine its approach, allocate resources more effectively, and adapt to emerging trends.

For example, if you notice that a particular issue is resonating strongly with voters in a specific area, this information can be relayed back to the campaign headquarters, prompting a strategic shift to emphasize that issue more heavily. Similarly, if you encounter common concerns or misconceptions about your candidate, the campaign can develop targeted messaging to address these issues.

Your mission as a doorknocker is multi-dimensional, encompassing persuasion, voter identification, mobilization, and data collection. By understanding and embracing these goals, you can approach each interaction with clarity and purpose, knowing that every door you knock on brings your candidate one step closer to victory.

## Understanding the Candidate's Platform and Key Issues

To effectively carry out your mission, it's essential to have a deep understanding of the candidate's platform and the key issues that define the campaign. Voters will have questions, concerns, and in some cases, doubts about your candidate, and your ability to respond knowledgeably and confidently will be critical to your success.

### 1. The Candidate's Platform: Core Beliefs and Policy Proposals

At the heart of any political campaign is the candidate's platform—the set of beliefs, values, and policy proposals that define what the candidate stands for and what they aim to achieve if elected. Understanding this platform is the foundation of your doorknocking efforts, as it informs every conversation you will have with voters.

Start by familiarizing yourself with the core principles and values that drive the candidate's campaign. These are often articulated in the candidate's speeches, campaign literature, and official website. What does the candidate stand for? What motivates their run for office? Understanding the "why" behind the candidate's platform will help you convey their message more authentically and persuasively.

Next, research the specific policy proposals that the candidate is advocating. These proposals will vary depending on the office being sought and the key issues in the election, but they typically cover a range of topics, such as healthcare, education, the economy, national security, and social justice. For each policy area, you should understand not only what the candidate proposes to do but also why they believe their approach is the best solution to the challenges facing the community or nation.

For example, if healthcare is a central issue in the campaign, you should be able to explain the candidate's plan to improve access to healthcare, reduce costs, or address specific challenges such as prescription drug prices. This might involve understanding the details of proposed legislation, the candidate's stance on existing policies (such as the Affordable Care Act), and how their proposals compare to those of their opponents.

In addition to policy specifics, it's important to understand how the candidate's platform aligns with the values and priorities of the electorate. This involves recognizing which issues are most important to the voters you will be engaging with and being able to articulate how the candidate's platform addresses those concerns.

## 2. Key Issues in the Campaign: What Matters Most to Voters?

While the candidate's platform provides the framework for your conversations, it's equally important to understand the key issues that are driving the election. These issues will vary depending on the political climate, the region, and the specific office being sought, but they typically reflect the concerns and priorities of the electorate.

To prepare for your doorknocking efforts, take the time to research and understand the major issues in the campaign. This might involve reading news articles, attending campaign events, and discussing the issues with other volunteers or campaign staff. Some common issues that often dominate political campaigns include:

- **Economy and Jobs**: Economic issues are often at the forefront of voters' minds, particularly in regions experiencing economic hardship. Be prepared to discuss the candidate's plans for job creation, economic growth, tax policy, and support for small businesses.

- **Healthcare**: Healthcare is a perennial issue in many campaigns, especially in light of ongoing debates over healthcare reform, access, and affordability. Understand the candidate's position on healthcare, including any specific proposals related to insurance coverage, prescription drug prices, and public health.

- **Education**: Education policy is a key concern for many voters, particularly those with children. Be familiar with the candidate's stance on issues such as school funding, teacher pay, student loan debt, and access to quality education.

- **National Security and Foreign Policy:** In races for federal office, national security and foreign policy are often major topics of discussion. Understand the candidate's approach to issues such as military spending, international alliances, and responses to global threats.

- **Social Justice and Civil Rights**: Social justice issues, including racial equality, LGBTQ+ rights, and criminal justice reform, are increasingly important to many voters. Know where the candidate stands on these issues and be prepared to discuss their proposals for advancing equality and justice.

- **Environment and Climate Change:** Environmental issues, particularly climate change, are a growing concern for many voters. Be ready to explain the candidate's position on environmental regulation, clean energy, and climate action.

- **Immigration**: Immigration policy remains a contentious issue in many campaigns. Understand the candidate's stance on border security, pathways to citizenship, refugee resettlement, and related issues.

As you prepare to discuss these key issues, remember that voters are often more concerned with how policies will affect them personally than with the details of legislative proposals. Be prepared to translate policy positions into tangible benefits for voters, explaining how the candidate's proposals will improve their lives, their communities, and their future.

**Tailoring Your Message to Different Voter Demographics**

One of the most important skills you will develop as a doorknocker is the ability to tailor your message to different voter demographics. Not all voters are the same, and the way you communicate with them should reflect their unique perspectives, concerns, and priorities. By understanding the diverse demographic groups in your community and adapting your message accordingly, you can increase the effectiveness of your outreach and build broader support for your candidate.

**1. Understanding Voter Demographics**

Voter demographics refer to the various characteristics that define different groups within the electorate. These characteristics can include age, gender, race and ethnicity, socioeconomic status, education level, religious affiliation, and more. Each demographic group may have different priorities and concerns, and they may respond differently to campaign messaging.

Before you begin doorknocking, take the time to research the demographics of the area you will be canvassing. This might involve reviewing voter data, analyzing census information, and discussing demographic trends with campaign staff.

Understanding the makeup of the community will help you anticipate the issues that are most important to different groups and tailor your approach accordingly.

For example, in a community with a large population of young voters, issues such as student loan debt, climate change, and social justice may be particularly resonant. In contrast, older voters may be more concerned with issues such as healthcare, retirement security, and public safety. By recognizing these differences, you can adjust your message to highlight the aspects of the candidate's platform that are most relevant to each demographic.

## 2. Tailoring Your Message: Key Considerations

When tailoring your message to different voter demographics, there are several key considerations to keep in mind:

- **Language and Tone:** The language and tone you use should be appropriate for the demographic you are engaging with. For example, when speaking with younger voters, a more informal and conversational tone may be effective, while older voters may appreciate a more respectful and formal approach. Additionally, if you are canvassing in a multilingual community, consider whether it would be beneficial to have materials available in multiple languages or to have bilingual volunteers on your team.

- **Emphasizing Relevant Issues:** Different demographic groups may prioritize different issues. When speaking with voters, focus on the issues that are most relevant to them. For example, when engaging with working-class voters, you might emphasize the candidate's plans for job creation and economic support. When speaking with parents, you might focus on education and childcare policies.

- **Building Trust and Rapport:** Building trust is essential to successful doorknocking, and this often involves finding common ground with voters. Take the time to understand the values and concerns of different demographic groups and look for ways to connect with them on a personal level. This might involve sharing stories or experiences that resonate with their background or expressing empathy for their concerns.

- **Addressing Specific Concerns:** Different demographic groups may have specific concerns or fears that need to be addressed. For example, minority communities may be concerned about issues of discrimination and civil rights, while rural voters may be focused on issues such as agricultural policy and access to healthcare. Be prepared to address these concerns directly and explain how the candidate's platform addresses them.

- **Respecting Cultural Differences:** When engaging with diverse communities, it's important to be respectful of cultural differences and traditions. This includes being aware of cultural norms and practices, as well as avoiding assumptions or stereotypes. Demonstrating cultural sensitivity can go a long way in building trust and rapport with voters from different backgrounds.

## 3. Engaging with Undecided and Swing Voters

Undecided and swing voters represent a critical demographic in any campaign, as they often hold the key to victory in closely contested races. These voters may be less ideologically committed than strong partisans and may be swayed by a variety of factors, including the candidate's personality, policy positions, and overall campaign message.

When engaging with undecided or swing voters, it's important to be flexible and responsive. These voters may have a range of concerns and priorities, and they may be seeking specific information or reassurance before making their decision. Your mission is to listen carefully to their concerns, provide clear and persuasive information, and help them see how your candidate aligns with their values and interests.

It's also important to recognize that undecided voters may be influenced by factors beyond policy positions, such as the candidate's character, leadership style, and ability to connect with people. In these cases, your role is to convey the candidate's strengths in these areas and to help the voter see the candidate as someone who understands their needs and will work on their behalf.

## The Importance of Listening and Responding to Voter Concerns

While much of your focus as a doorknocker will be on delivering the campaign's message and persuading voters to support your candidate, it's equally important to remember the power of listening. Listening to voters is not only a key part of effective communication but also an essential aspect of building trust, understanding voter concerns, and ultimately winning their support.

## 1. Active Listening: What It Is and Why It Matters

Active listening is the practice of fully engaging with the person you are speaking to, paying close attention to their words, tone, and body language, and responding in a way that shows you understand and care about what they are saying. In the context of doorknocking, active listening involves more than just hearing what voters have to say; it means genuinely trying to understand their concerns, values, and motivations.

Active listening is important for several reasons:

- **Building Trust**: When voters feel that you are truly listening to them, they are more likely to trust you and, by extension, your candidate. This trust is crucial to building support and persuading undecided voters.

- **Gaining Insights:** Listening to voters provides valuable insights into their concerns, priorities, and perceptions of the campaign. This information can inform your conversations and help the campaign refine its messaging.

- **Demonstrating Empathy:** Voters want to feel that their concerns are being taken seriously. By listening carefully and responding empathetically, you demonstrate that the campaign values their input and is committed to addressing their needs.

- **Creating a Positive Experience:** A positive, respectful interaction at the doorstep can leave a lasting impression, even if the voter does not immediately commit to supporting your candidate. By listening attentively and responding thoughtfully, you can create a positive experience that may influence the voter's decision later on.

## 2. Responding to Voter Concerns: Strategies and Tips

Responding effectively to voter concerns requires a combination of knowledge, empathy, and communication skills. Here are some strategies and tips for addressing the concerns that voters may raise during your doorknocking efforts:

- **Acknowledge the Concern**: The first step in responding to a voter's concern is to acknowledge it. This shows that you are listening and that you take their concerns seriously. For example, if a voter expresses frustration with the current state of healthcare, you might say, "I understand that healthcare is a major concern for many people, and it's something our candidate is deeply committed to improving."

- **Provide Relevant Information**: Once you have acknowledged the concern, provide relevant information about how your candidate's platform addresses the issue. Be clear, concise, and specific, focusing on how the candidate's policies will directly benefit the voter. For example, you might explain, "Our candidate has proposed a plan to lower prescription drug costs and expand access to affordable healthcare, which will help ensure that everyone can get the care they need."

- **Address Misconceptions:** Voters may have misconceptions or misunderstandings about the candidate or their policies.

If you encounter a voter who is misinformed, take the time to clarify the issue in a respectful and non-confrontational manner. For example, if a voter believes a false rumor about the candidate, you might say, "I can understand why you might have concerns, but I'd like to clarify that our candidate has consistently supported policies that protect [specific issue]."

- **Empathize with Their Situation:** Empathy is a powerful tool in building rapport with voters. If a voter shares a personal story or expresses deep concerns, take the time to empathize with their situation. For example, if a voter is worried about job security, you might say, "I can imagine how stressful that must be. Our candidate is focused on creating good-paying jobs and supporting workers in our community."

- **Offer to Follow Up:** If a voter has a complex question or concern that you cannot fully address at the moment, offer to follow up with more information. This could involve providing them with campaign literature, directing them to the candidate's website, or offering to have someone from the campaign contact them with more details. This shows that you are committed to addressing their concerns and providing them with the information they need to make an informed decision.

- **Stay Positive and Respectful:** Even if a voter is skeptical or critical, it's important to remain positive and respectful throughout the conversation. Avoid getting defensive or argumentative, and instead, focus on finding common ground and providing constructive responses. Remember, your goal is to leave the voter with a positive impression of the candidate and the campaign.

- **Know When to Move On:** Not every conversation will end with a voter fully persuaded or satisfied, and that's okay. If a voter remains resistant or uninterested, it's important to know when to politely move on. Thank them for their time, leave them with campaign literature if appropriate, and move on to the next door. Every interaction is valuable, but not every voter will be receptive, and that's part of the process.

## The Mission is the Message

Understanding your mission as a doorknocker is about more than just delivering talking points and collecting data. It's about engaging with voters on a personal level, understanding their concerns, and building trust in your candidate. By defining your goals, understanding the candidate's platform, tailoring your message to different voter demographics, and practicing active listening, you can make a meaningful impact on the campaign and help move your candidate closer to victory.

As you continue your doorknocking efforts, keep in mind that every interaction, no matter how brief, is an opportunity to advance your mission. Whether you're persuading an undecided voter, mobilizing a supporter, or gathering valuable feedback, your work at the doorstep is a vital part of the campaign's success. Approach each door with confidence, empathy, and a clear sense of purpose, knowing that you are playing a crucial role in the democratic process.

# Chapter 3: Mapping Out Your Territory

In the complex and fast-paced world of political campaigning, one of the most critical tasks you will undertake as a doorknocker is mapping out your territory. Effective doorknocking is not just about knocking on as many doors as possible; it's about strategic targeting—choosing the right neighborhoods and precincts, reaching the voters who matter most, and making every interaction count.

## How to Choose the Right Neighborhoods and Precincts to Target

The first step in mapping out your territory is selecting the neighborhoods and precincts where you will focus your efforts. This decision is not arbitrary; it requires a careful analysis of various factors, including voter demographics, historical voting patterns, and the specific goals of your campaign. By targeting the right areas, you can maximize the impact of your doorknocking and help drive your candidate to victory.

### 1. Understanding Your Campaign's Goals

Before you can choose the right neighborhoods and precincts, it's important to have a clear understanding of your campaign's goals. These goals will influence where you should focus your efforts. For example, if your primary objective is to persuade undecided voters, you'll want to target areas with a high concentration of swing voters. If your goal is to mobilize your base and ensure high voter turnout, you'll focus on neighborhoods where your candidate already has strong support.

Campaigns typically have a variety of goals that might include:

- **Voter Persuasion**: Targeting undecided or swing voters who could be persuaded to support your candidate.

- **Voter Identification**: Identifying potential supporters and gathering data on their preferences and concerns.

- **Voter Mobilization**: Ensuring that supporters turn out to vote, particularly in areas with historically low turnout.

- **Issue Advocacy:** Focusing on neighborhoods where specific issues resonate strongly with voters.

Each of these goals requires a different approach to territory mapping, so be sure to align your efforts with the overarching strategy of the campaign.

## 2. Analyzing Voter Demographics

Voter demographics play a crucial role in determining where you should focus your doorknocking efforts. Different demographic groups may have different priorities, concerns, and voting behaviors, so understanding the makeup of the neighborhoods you are targeting is essential.

Some key demographic factors to consider include:

- **Age**: Younger voters may be more concerned with issues like climate change, student debt, and social justice, while older voters may prioritize healthcare, retirement security, and public safety.

- **Income**: Economic issues often resonate differently with voters depending on their income level. Working-class neighborhoods may be more focused on job creation and wage growth, while affluent areas may be more concerned with tax policy and economic stability.

- **Race and Ethnicity**: Minority communities may have specific concerns related to civil rights, immigration, and social justice. Understanding the racial and ethnic makeup of a neighborhood can help you tailor your message accordingly.

- **Education Level:** Voters with higher levels of education may be more engaged with complex policy issues, while those with less formal education may prioritize more immediate concerns like job security and healthcare.

- **Political Affiliation:** While doorknocking is often focused on persuading undecided voters, it's also important to consider the political leanings of a neighborhood. Areas with a high concentration of voters who share your candidate's party affiliation may be ideal for voter mobilization efforts.

To analyze voter demographics, you can use a variety of tools and resources, including census data, voter rolls, and polling data. Many campaigns also have access to proprietary databases that provide detailed demographic information about voters in specific areas. By combining this data with your understanding of the campaign's goals, you can identify the neighborhoods and precincts that are most likely to yield positive results.

## 3. Historical Voting Patterns

Another important factor to consider when choosing where to doorknock is the historical voting patterns of the area. Understanding how a neighborhood or precinct has voted in past elections can provide valuable insights into its political landscape and help you prioritize your efforts.

Some key questions to ask when analyzing historical voting patterns include:

- **How did this area vote in the last election?** If the neighborhood or precinct has consistently supported your candidate's party, it may be a stronghold where you can focus on voter mobilization. If it has leaned toward the opposition, it may be an area where voter persuasion is more critical.

- **What is the voter turnout in this area?** Areas with low voter turnout may be ripe for mobilization efforts, especially if they have a high concentration of potential supporters. Conversely, areas with high turnout may require less focus, particularly if the votes are already likely to go in your favor.

- **Has the area shown signs of political realignment?** Some neighborhoods and precincts may be in the process of shifting their political allegiances. Understanding these trends can help you identify swing areas that could be pivotal in the election.

Historical voting data can often be obtained from local election boards, political data firms, and campaign databases. By analyzing this data in conjunction with voter demographics, you can make informed decisions about where to focus your doorknocking efforts.

## 4. Geographic Considerations

In addition to demographic and historical factors, it's important to consider the geographic layout of the neighborhoods and precincts you plan to target. Geography can impact the logistics of your doorknocking efforts, including the time it takes to cover an area, the accessibility of different neighborhoods, and the overall efficiency of your route.

Some geographic considerations to keep in mind include:

- **Density**: Urban areas with high population density allow you to reach more voters in a shorter amount of time, making them ideal for concentrated doorknocking efforts. However, these areas may also require more careful planning to navigate apartment buildings, gated communities, and other obstacles.

- **Transportation**: Consider how easy it is to travel to and within the neighborhoods you are targeting. If you're working in a rural area or a large suburban precinct, you may need to account for longer travel times and plan your routes accordingly.

- **Physical Barriers:** Natural features like rivers, hills, and highways can create physical barriers that make some areas more difficult to reach. Be sure to account for these barriers when mapping out your routes.

- **Safety**: Always consider the safety of the neighborhoods you are targeting. If an area has a high crime rate or other safety concerns, it may be advisable to avoid doorknocking there or to take additional precautions, such as canvassing in pairs.

By taking these geographic factors into account, you can optimize your doorknocking efforts and ensure that you are reaching as many voters as possible in the most efficient and effective way.

## Using Data and Voter Rolls to Plan Your Routes

Once you have identified the neighborhoods and precincts you want to target, the next step is to plan your doorknocking routes. This process involves using data and voter rolls to map out the most efficient and effective paths through your target areas, ensuring that you reach the right voters with the right message.

## 1. What Are Voter Rolls?

Voter rolls, also known as voter registration lists, are databases that contain information about registered voters in a given area. These lists typically include details such as the voter's name, address, party affiliation, and voting history. Voter rolls are a valuable resource for campaigns because they provide the foundational data needed to plan doorknocking efforts.

Access to voter rolls can vary depending on the state and local election laws. In many cases, voter rolls are available to political campaigns, parties, and organizations for a fee. The data can be used to identify potential supporters, target swing voters, and prioritize areas for doorknocking.

## 2. Segmenting Voters: Identifying Your Targets

The first step in using voter rolls is to segment the electorate based on the campaign's goals. This process involves categorizing voters into different groups according to factors such as party affiliation, voting history, and demographics. Common voter segments include:

- **Strong Supporters:** Voters who are likely to support your candidate based on their party affiliation, past voting behavior, or other indicators. These voters are prime targets for mobilization efforts.

- **Leaners:** Voters who are inclined to support your candidate but may not be fully committed. These voters are important targets for persuasion efforts, as they can be swayed with the right message.

- **Undecided Voters:** Voters who have not yet made up their minds about which candidate to support. These voters are critical targets for persuasion, as they represent a significant opportunity to gain new supporters.

- **Opposition:** Voters who are likely to support the opposing candidate or party. While these voters are not typically the focus of doorknocking efforts, it's important to be aware of their presence and to approach them with a respectful and non-confrontational attitude.

Once you have segmented the voters in your target areas, you can use this information to prioritize your efforts. For example, you might choose to focus on areas with a high concentration of leaners and undecided voters, while devoting less time to areas dominated by opposition voters.

## 3. Using Data to Plan Your Routes

With your voter segments identified, the next step is to plan your doorknocking routes. This process involves mapping out the most efficient paths through your target neighborhoods and precincts, ensuring that you reach as many voters as possible in the time available.

There are several tools and techniques you can use to plan your routes:

- **Mapping Software:** Many campaigns use specialized mapping software that integrates voter roll data with geographic information systems (GIS). These tools allow you to visualize your target areas, identify clusters of voters, and create optimized routes that minimize travel time and maximize voter contact.

- **Canvassing Apps:** In recent years, canvassing apps have become an increasingly popular tool for doorknocking. These apps allow you to access voter data, track your progress, and record the results of your interactions in real-time. Some apps also offer route optimization features that help you plan the most efficient paths through your target areas.

- **Manual Mapping:** While digital tools are highly effective, some campaigns may prefer a more hands-on approach to route planning. This can involve printing out maps of your target areas, marking the locations of key voter segments, and manually drawing your routes. While this method can be time-consuming, it allows for a high degree of customization and flexibility.

When planning your routes, be sure to consider factors such as:

- **Voter Density:** Focus on areas with a high concentration of your target voter segments. This will allow you to reach more voters in less time and maximize the impact of your efforts.

- **Geographic Efficiency:** Plan routes that minimize backtracking and unnecessary travel. This will help you cover more ground and reach more voters in the time available.

- **Time of Day:** Consider the time of day when planning your routes. Some voters may be more likely to be home in the evening, while others may be available during the day. Be sure to adjust your routes accordingly to maximize voter contact.

- **Weather and Terrain:** Take into account the weather and terrain of your target areas. For example, if you are doorknocking in a hilly or rural area, you may need to adjust your routes to account for longer travel times and more challenging conditions.

By using data and voter rolls to plan your routes, you can ensure that your doorknocking efforts are as efficient and effective as possible, allowing you to reach the right voters with the right message.

## Prioritizing High-Impact Areas: Swing Voters, Undecided Voters, and Supporters

Not all voters are created equal when it comes to the impact they can have on an election. Some voters are firmly committed to your candidate, while others are undecided or leaning toward the opposition. To maximize the effectiveness of your doorknocking efforts, it's important to prioritize the areas where you can have the greatest impact—specifically, those with high concentrations of swing voters, undecided voters, and supporters.

## 1. The Importance of Swing Voters

Swing voters—those who are not firmly committed to any one candidate or party—are often the key to winning elections, especially in competitive races. These voters can be persuaded to support your candidate with the right message, making them a high-priority target for doorknocking efforts.

Swing voters are typically identified through a combination of voter roll data, polling, and historical voting patterns. They may be registered as independents, have a history of voting for candidates from different parties, or have expressed uncertainty about their voting preferences in surveys or conversations.

When targeting swing voters, it's important to focus on personalized, persuasive messaging that addresses their specific concerns and priorities. These voters may be more open to discussion and more likely to be swayed by a thoughtful, respectful conversation. Be prepared to listen carefully to their concerns, provide clear and relevant information about your candidate's platform, and address any doubts they may have.

## 2. Undecided Voters: The Key to Expanding Your Base

Undecided voters represent another critical target for doorknocking efforts. These voters have not yet made up their minds about which candidate to support, and they may be receptive to new information and persuasive arguments. Like swing voters, undecided voters can be identified through voter rolls, polling, and other data sources.

To reach undecided voters, prioritize areas where they are most likely to be found, such as neighborhoods with a mix of party affiliations or areas with a history of political volatility. When engaging with undecided voters, focus on understanding their concerns and providing information that directly addresses their questions and doubts.

One effective strategy for persuading undecided voters is to emphasize the candidate's strengths in areas that resonate with the voter's personal values and interests. For example, if a voter is particularly concerned about healthcare, focus on the candidate's healthcare policies and how they will benefit the voter and their community. Additionally, sharing personal stories or examples of how the candidate has positively impacted others can help create a connection and build trust.

## 3. Mobilizing Supporters: Turning Enthusiasm into Votes

# KNOCKING ON DEMOCRACY'S DOOR

While persuading swing and undecided voters is crucial, it's equally important to focus on mobilizing your existing supporters. These voters are already inclined to support your candidate, but their vote only counts if they actually show up on election day. Ensuring that your supporters are informed, motivated, and prepared to vote is a key part of your doorknocking mission.

When targeting supporters, prioritize areas where your candidate has a strong base, such as neighborhoods with high concentrations of registered voters from your candidate's party. Your goal in these areas is to solidify their commitment, provide them with any information they need to vote (such as polling locations and voting hours), and encourage them to spread the word to their friends and family.

In addition to encouraging voter turnout, you can also use your interactions with supporters to recruit volunteers, distribute campaign materials, and gather feedback that can be used to improve the campaign's strategy. Supporters who feel engaged and valued are more likely to become active participants in the campaign, further amplifying your efforts.

## Staying Organized: Tools and Apps to Track Your Progress

Effective doorknocking requires more than just a well-planned route and a persuasive message; it also requires staying organized and tracking your progress. By using the right tools and apps, you can ensure that your efforts are efficient, data-driven, and continuously improving.

## 1. Canvassing Apps: The Modern Toolbox

In recent years, canvassing apps have revolutionized the way political campaigns conduct doorknocking. These apps provide a range of features that streamline the process, including:

- **Voter Data Access**: Canvassing apps allow you to access voter data in real-time, including information about the voters you are targeting, their voting history, and any notes from previous interactions. This helps you tailor your approach and ensures that you are reaching the right people with the right message.

- **Route Optimization:** Many canvassing apps offer route optimization features that help you plan the most efficient paths through your target areas. This saves time and allows you to reach more voters in a single session.

- **Progress Tracking**: Canvassing apps enable you to track your progress as you doorknock, including the number of doors you have knocked on, the number of voters you have spoken to, and the results of those interactions. This data is invaluable for assessing the effectiveness of your efforts and making adjustments as needed.

- **Data Entry and Reporting:** After each interaction, you can use the app to record notes, update voter information, and report back to the campaign headquarters. This ensures that the data you collect is immediately available for analysis and follow-up.

- **Communication**: Some canvassing apps include communication features that allow you to stay in touch with your team, receive updates from the campaign, and report any issues or concerns in real-time.

Popular canvassing apps used by political campaigns include Minivan, Ecanvasser, and VoterCircle. Each app offers a different set of features, so it's important to choose the one that best fits the needs of your campaign.

## 2. Spreadsheets and Databases: Tracking and Analyzing Data

While canvassing apps are powerful tools, some campaigns may also use spreadsheets and databases to track and analyze data. These tools offer a high degree of customization and flexibility, allowing you to organize and analyze voter information in a way that best suits your needs.

- **Spreadsheets**: Spreadsheets such as Microsoft Excel or Google Sheets can be used to track voter interactions, record notes, and analyze data. For example, you might use a spreadsheet to create a list of voters in a specific neighborhood, categorize them by their level of support, and track the results of your doorknocking efforts. Spreadsheets are particularly useful for organizing large amounts of data and performing complex analyses.

- **Databases**: Databases such as Microsoft Access or custom-built solutions can be used to store and manage voter data on a larger scale. Databases allow for more sophisticated data management, including the ability to search, filter, and cross-reference voter information. They are especially useful for campaigns with large voter rolls and multiple canvassing teams.

Whether you use a canvassing app, a spreadsheet, or a database, the key is to stay organized and ensure that your data is accurate, up-to-date, and easily accessible. This will enable you to track your progress, identify trends, and make data-driven decisions that enhance the effectiveness of your doorknocking efforts.

### 3. Reporting and Feedback: Continuous Improvement

One of the most important aspects of staying organized is the ability to report your progress and provide feedback to the campaign headquarters. This allows the campaign to track the overall success of the doorknocking efforts, identify areas for improvement, and make strategic adjustments as needed.

When reporting your progress, be sure to include the following information:

- **Number of Doors Knocked:** The total number of doors you have knocked on in a given area. This helps the campaign gauge the reach of your efforts.

- **Voter Interactions:** The number of voters you have spoken to and the results of those interactions (e.g., persuaded, undecided, supporter).

- **Voter Feedback:** Any feedback you have received from voters, including their concerns, priorities, and perceptions of the candidate. This information is valuable for refining the campaign's messaging and strategy.

- **Challenges and Issues:** Any challenges or issues you encountered while doorknocking, such as difficulties accessing certain neighborhoods, negative voter reactions, or logistical problems. Reporting these issues allows the campaign to address them and provide support where needed.

In addition to formal reporting, consider providing informal feedback to your campaign team. Sharing your experiences, observations, and insights can help the campaign identify new opportunities, improve its approach, and ultimately increase its chances of success.

## Mapping the Path to Victory

Mapping out your territory is one of the most critical components of a successful doorknocking campaign. By choosing the right neighborhoods and precincts to target, using data and voter rolls to plan your routes, prioritizing high-impact areas, and staying organized with the right tools and apps, you can maximize the effectiveness of your efforts and help drive your candidate to victory.

Remember, doorknocking is not just about quantity; it's about quality. Every interaction you have with a voter is an opportunity to persuade, mobilize, and build support. By approaching your doorknocking efforts with a strategic mindset and a clear sense of purpose, you can make a meaningful difference in the outcome of the election.

As you continue your doorknocking journey, keep in mind that every step you take, every door you knock on, and every conversation you have is part of a larger mission to engage voters, build relationships, and create positive change in your community. Stay focused, stay organized, and stay committed to your mission, knowing that your work is helping to shape the future of your candidate, your community, and your country.

# Chapter 4: The Art of the Approach

The first few moments of a doorknocking interaction are critical. They set the tone for the entire conversation and can determine whether a voter is receptive to your message or closes the door on you—literally and figuratively. Mastering the art of the approach involves more than just knocking on a door; it requires understanding how to make a great first impression, knowing when to be assertive or friendly, effectively handling different types of voters, and using icebreakers and conversation starters that engage and interest the voter.

**How to Make a Great First Impression**

Making a great first impression is crucial in doorknocking because you often have just a few seconds to capture a voter's attention and earn their trust. A strong first impression can open the door to a productive conversation, while a poor one can shut it down before it even begins. Here's how to ensure that your first impression leaves a positive mark:

**1. Appearance Matters**

The way you present yourself at the doorstep can significantly influence how voters perceive you and, by extension, your candidate. While it's important to be yourself, there are some general guidelines for ensuring that your appearance helps, rather than hinders, your doorknocking efforts:

- **Dress Appropriately:** Your clothing should be professional but comfortable. Aim for a business-casual look that reflects the seriousness of your mission but also allows you to move freely and stay comfortable throughout the day. Avoid clothing that is too casual (such as shorts, flip-flops, or overly flashy attire) or too formal (such as a suit and tie, unless the situation calls for it).

- **Consider the Community:** Tailor your appearance to the community you're visiting. If you're canvassing in a working-class neighborhood, dressing down slightly may help you relate better to the voters. In more affluent areas, a slightly more polished look might be appropriate. In all cases, avoid anything that might come across as intimidating or out of touch with the community.

- **Wear Campaign Gear:** If your campaign provides t-shirts, buttons, or hats with the candidate's logo, wearing them can help establish your credibility and make it clear that you are a representative of the campaign. However, make sure that any campaign gear is clean, in good condition, and appropriate for the setting.

- **Personal Grooming:** Ensure that you are well-groomed. This means clean hair, a neat shave (if applicable), and fresh breath. These small details can make a big difference in how you are perceived.

## 2. Body Language and Posture

Your body language communicates just as much—if not more—than your words. Positive body language can make you seem approachable, trustworthy, and confident, while negative body language can create barriers and make voters wary.

- **Stand Tall and Confident:** Your posture should be upright and confident. Slouching or appearing tense can make you seem uncertain or uncomfortable, which can be off-putting to voters.

- **Smile Genuinely:** A warm, genuine smile is one of the most powerful tools in making a great first impression. It shows that you are friendly, approachable, and happy to be there. Smiling can also help put voters at ease, making them more receptive to your message.

- **Make Eye Contact:** Eye contact is crucial in building trust and rapport. When the voter answers the door, make sure to make eye contact as you introduce yourself. This shows that you are confident and sincere. However, be careful not to overdo it, as too much eye contact can come across as intense or aggressive.

- **Mind Your Gestures:** Your gestures should be open and inviting. Avoid crossing your arms, which can make you seem closed off or defensive. Instead, use open-handed gestures that convey friendliness and transparency.

### 3. Tone of Voice

The tone of your voice can also have a significant impact on how voters perceive you. It's important to strike the right balance between being confident and approachable:

- **Be Clear and Articulate:** Speak clearly and at a moderate pace. Mumbling or speaking too quickly can make it difficult for voters to understand you, while speaking too slowly can come across as patronizing.

- **Use a Warm, Friendly Tone:** Your tone should be warm and friendly, without being overly casual. A friendly tone helps put voters at ease and makes them more likely to engage in conversation. However, avoid sounding overly familiar or informal, as this can be off-putting, especially with voters who value professionalism.

- **Adjust Your Volume:** Be mindful of your volume. You want to speak loudly enough to be heard, but not so loud that it feels intrusive or aggressive. If you're in a quiet neighborhood, a softer tone might be appropriate; in a noisier environment, you may need to raise your voice slightly.

### 4. The Power of a Polite Introduction

Your introduction is your first verbal interaction with the voter and sets the tone for the entire conversation. A polite, well-crafted introduction can help establish rapport and open the door to a meaningful discussion.

- **Start with a Greeting:** Begin with a simple, polite greeting such as "Good afternoon" or "Hello." This sets a positive tone and acknowledges the voter's presence.

- **Introduce Yourself:** Clearly state your name and your affiliation with the campaign. For example, "My name is [Your

Name], and I'm a volunteer with [Candidate's Name]'s campaign."

- **State Your Purpose:** Briefly explain why you're there. For example, "I'm here today to talk to you about the upcoming election and to share a little bit about [Candidate's Name] and what they stand for." Keep it short and to the point; the goal is to pique the voter's interest without overwhelming them with information right away.

## 5. Reading the Voter's Reaction

As you deliver your introduction, pay close attention to the voter's reaction. Their body language, facial expressions, and tone of voice can provide valuable clues about how they feel and how you should proceed:

- **Positive or Neutral Reaction:** If the voter responds with a smile, a nod, or a polite acknowledgment, this is a good sign that they are open to conversation. In this case, you can proceed with your message and begin engaging them in discussion.

- **Cautious or Hesitant Reaction:** If the voter seems hesitant, confused, or cautious, it may be helpful to pause and give them a moment to respond. You might also offer a brief reassurance, such as "I'll just take a minute of your time," to put them at ease.

- **Negative or Defensive Reaction:** If the voter crosses their arms, frowns, or responds in a curt or defensive manner, it's important to proceed with caution. In this case, you may want to adjust your approach by asking a question or addressing any concerns they might have right away. It's crucial to remain polite and respectful, even if the voter seems disinterested or hostile.

## Strategies for Knocking on Doors: When to Be Assertive vs. Friendly

Every voter is different, and there's no one-size-fits-all approach to doorknocking. Knowing when to be assertive and when to adopt a more friendly, laid-back approach is key to having productive conversations and achieving your campaign goals.

### 1. Understanding Assertiveness in Doorknocking

Being assertive in the context of doorknocking doesn't mean being pushy or aggressive. Instead, it means being confident, clear, and purposeful in your interactions. Assertiveness is about taking control of the conversation in a way that is respectful but firm, ensuring that your message is heard and that you guide the discussion toward your campaign's goals.

Situations where assertiveness might be appropriate include:

- Short Interactions: When you know you have limited time (for example, if the voter indicates they are in a hurry), being assertive can help you deliver your key points quickly and efficiently. This might involve cutting straight to the most important information and politely but firmly steering the conversation to its conclusion.

- Handling Tough Questions: If a voter challenges you with a tough question or expresses doubts about your candidate, assertiveness can help you maintain control of the conversation. This involves addressing the question directly, providing clear and confident answers, and guiding the discussion back to your key messages.

- Engaging Indifferent Voters: When dealing with voters who seem indifferent or apathetic, a more assertive approach can sometimes help spark their interest. This might involve confidently highlighting the stakes of the election and explaining why their vote is important.

## 2. Understanding Friendliness in Doorknocking

A friendly approach is about building rapport, making the voter feel comfortable, and creating a positive, relaxed atmosphere for conversation. Friendliness is especially important when trying to build trust, relate to the voter on a personal level, or when you sense that the voter might be open to a more casual discussion.

Situations where a friendly approach might be appropriate include:

- **Longer Conversations**: When the voter seems interested and willing to engage in a longer conversation, a friendly approach can help build a deeper connection. This might involve sharing personal anecdotes, asking the voter about their own experiences, and taking the time to listen to their concerns.

- **Engaging Supporters:** When speaking with voters who already support your candidate, a friendly approach can help reinforce their commitment and encourage them to take further action, such as volunteering or encouraging others to vote.

- **Building Trust with Undecided Voters:** When dealing with undecided voters who are still making up their minds, a friendly approach can help you build trust and establish a connection that may influence their decision.

## 3. Balancing Assertiveness and Friendliness

The most effective doorknockers are those who can seamlessly switch between assertiveness and friendliness depending on the situation. Here are some tips for finding the right balance:

- **Read the Situation:** Pay attention to the voter's cues—both verbal and non-verbal. If the voter seems engaged and open, a friendly approach might be most effective. If they seem pressed for time or unsure, a more assertive approach might be needed to ensure you get your key points across.

- **Start Friendly, Then Adjust:** In most cases, it's a good idea to start with a friendly approach. This helps build rapport and puts the voter at ease. If the conversation becomes more challenging or if time is limited, you can shift to a more assertive tone to guide the discussion.

- **Stay Respectful:** Whether you're being assertive or friendly, always maintain a respectful and courteous demeanor. Assertiveness should never cross the line into aggressiveness, and friendliness should never come across as insincere or flippant.

## Handling Different Types of Voters: Enthusiastic, Indifferent, or Hostile

As a doorknocker, you will encounter a wide range of voter attitudes and responses. Some voters will be enthusiastic and eager to engage, while others may be indifferent, apathetic, or even hostile. Knowing how to handle each type of voter is crucial to maximizing the impact of your doorknocking efforts.

### 1. Engaging Enthusiastic Voters

Enthusiastic voters are those who are already excited about your candidate or cause. They may be familiar with the campaign, supportive of the candidate, and eager to engage in conversation. These voters are often your strongest allies, and they can play a key role in helping you spread the campaign's message.

Here's how to handle enthusiastic voters:

- **Reinforce Their Commitment:** Express appreciation for their support and reinforce their commitment to the campaign. You might say something like, "Thank you so much for your support! It's voters like you who make a real difference in this election."

- **Provide Additional Information:** Enthusiastic voters often want to know how they can get more involved. Provide them with information about upcoming events, volunteer opportunities, or ways to spread the word to friends and family. This could include handing out campaign literature, signing them up for campaign updates, or inviting them to join a canvassing team.

- **Leverage Their Enthusiasm:** Encourage enthusiastic voters to take action beyond just voting. Ask if they would be willing to volunteer, host a campaign event, or share information on social media. Their enthusiasm can be a powerful tool in mobilizing others.

- **Listen to Their Ideas:** Enthusiastic voters often have ideas and suggestions for the campaign. Take the time to listen to their thoughts, and if appropriate, pass their feedback along to the campaign team. This not only makes them feel valued but also helps the campaign stay connected with its supporters.

## 2. Engaging Indifferent or Apathetic Voters

Indifferent or apathetic voters are those who are either uninterested in the election or skeptical about the importance of voting. They may feel that their vote doesn't matter, that all politicians are the same, or that the issues don't affect them personally. Engaging these voters can be challenging, but it's also an opportunity to expand the campaign's base of support.

Here's how to handle indifferent or apathetic voters:

- **Connect with Their Values:** Try to find a way to connect the campaign's message with the voter's personal values or interests. Ask open-ended questions to learn more about what matters to them, and then explain how the candidate's platform aligns with those values. For example, "I understand you're not really interested in politics, but how do you feel about [specific issue]? Our candidate has a plan that could really make a difference in that area."

- **Highlight the Stakes:** Emphasize the importance of the election and the potential consequences of not participating. This might involve explaining the impact of local policies on their daily life or discussing how their vote could influence the outcome in a close race. "I know it can feel like one vote doesn't make a difference, but in a close race like this, every vote really does count."

- **Keep It Short and Simple:** Indifferent voters may not be interested in a long conversation, so keep your message short, simple, and to the point. Focus on one or two key issues that are most likely to resonate with them, and avoid overwhelming them with too much information.

- **Offer to Follow Up:** If the voter seems somewhat interested but not fully convinced, offer to provide more information or follow up at a later time. This could involve leaving campaign literature, directing them to the campaign's website, or offering to answer any questions they may have in the future.

## 3. Handling Hostile or Opposed Voters

Hostile voters are those who are opposed to your candidate or who may have strong negative feelings about politics in general. These voters can be challenging to engage, and in some cases, it may be best to avoid confrontation and move on. However, if you choose to engage, it's important to do so with care, respect, and diplomacy.

Here's how to handle hostile or opposed voters:

- **Stay Calm and Respectful:** The most important thing to remember when dealing with hostile voters is to stay calm and respectful. Avoid getting defensive or argumentative, even if the voter is confrontational. A calm, respectful demeanor can help de-escalate the situation and prevent the conversation from becoming heated.

- **Acknowledge Their Concerns:** Start by acknowledging the voter's concerns, even if you don't agree with them. This shows that you respect their opinion and are willing to listen. For example, "I understand that you have strong feelings about this issue, and I appreciate you sharing your perspective."

- **Find Common Ground:** If possible, try to find some common ground with the voter. This could involve identifying a shared value, concern, or interest. For example, "While we may disagree on this issue, I think we both want what's best for our community."

- **Know When to Disengage:** Sometimes, the best approach with a hostile voter is to politely disengage and move on. If the voter is not open to discussion or if the conversation becomes too confrontational, it's okay to thank them for their time and move on to the next door. "I appreciate your time and understand where you're coming from. Thank you for sharing your thoughts, and have a good day."

**Icebreakers and Conversation Starters**

# KNOCKING ON DEMOCRACY'S DOOR

The first few moments of a conversation can be the most challenging, especially when you're trying to engage a voter who may not be expecting you. Icebreakers and conversation starters are essential tools for breaking the ice, capturing the voter's attention, and steering the conversation in a productive direction.

## 1. The Purpose of Icebreakers

Icebreakers serve several important purposes in doorknocking:

- **Put the Voter at Ease:** An effective icebreaker can help put the voter at ease, making them more receptive to your message. It breaks down initial barriers and creates a more relaxed atmosphere for conversation.

- **Gauge Interest:** Icebreakers can also help you gauge the voter's level of interest and engagement. Depending on how they respond, you can adjust your approach accordingly.

- **Transition into the Conversation:** Icebreakers provide a natural transition into the main part of your conversation, helping you move smoothly from the introduction to the discussion of key issues.

## 2. Effective Icebreakers

Here are some effective icebreakers and conversation starters you can use when doorknocking:

- **Compliment the Voter's Home or Garden:** A genuine compliment about the voter's home, garden, or neighborhood can be a great way to start the conversation. For example, "You have a beautiful garden! How long have you been living in this neighborhood?" This not only breaks the ice but also shows that you're paying attention and appreciate their surroundings.

- **Mention a Local Event or Issue:** Referring to a recent local event or issue that the voter might be aware of can be an effective way to start the conversation. For example, "Did you hear about the recent town hall meeting on [issue]? Our candidate has been really involved in that." This helps establish common ground and signals that you're informed and engaged with the community.

- **Ask a Question:** Asking an open-ended question is a great way to engage the voter and get them talking. For example, "What are some of the issues that are most important to you in this upcoming election?" or "How do you feel about the direction our community is heading?" This invites the voter to share their thoughts and opens the door for a deeper conversation.

- **Share a Personal Story:** Sharing a brief personal story or experience related to the campaign can be a powerful way to connect with the voter. For example, "I've been volunteering with [Candidate's Name] because I really believe in their plan for improving our schools. As a parent, that's something that's really important to me." This helps humanize the campaign and shows that you have a personal stake in the issues.

- **Express Gratitude:** Simply expressing gratitude for the voter's time and willingness to listen can be an effective icebreaker. For example, "I really appreciate you taking a moment to chat with me today. It means a lot to know that people like you are engaged in our community." This sets a positive tone and helps build rapport.

**3. Tailoring Icebreakers to the Voter**

It's important to tailor your icebreakers and conversation starters to the specific voter you're engaging with. Here are some tips for doing so:

- **Consider the Voter's Demographics:** Tailor your icebreakers to the voter's age, background, and interests. For example, if you're speaking with a young parent, a comment about local schools or playgrounds might resonate. If you're speaking with an older voter, a reference to local history or community events might be more effective.

- **Adapt to the Voter's Mood:** Pay attention to the voter's mood and demeanor when they answer the door. If they seem rushed or distracted, a quick, direct icebreaker might be best. If they seem relaxed and open, you can use a more casual or conversational icebreaker.

- **Use Visual Cues:** Look for visual cues around the voter's home that might suggest a good icebreaker. For example, a "Support Our Troops" sign might prompt you to ask about their thoughts on national security, while a garden full of flowers might lead to a compliment on their gardening skills.

**Mastering the Art of the Approach**

The art of the approach in doorknocking is about more than just delivering a message; it's about making a strong first impression, knowing when to be assertive or friendly, effectively handling different types of voters, and using icebreakers to engage and interest the voter. By mastering these skills, you can increase your effectiveness as a doorknocker, build stronger connections with voters, and ultimately contribute to the success of your campaign.

As you continue to hone your approach, remember that every interaction is an opportunity to learn and improve. Pay attention to what works and what doesn't, and be willing to adapt your strategy as needed. With practice and persistence, you can become a more confident and effective doorknocker, capable of making a meaningful impact in your community and helping to shape the outcome of the election.

# Chapter 5: Handling Common Challenges

Doorknocking is one of the most effective ways to engage with voters and drive a political campaign forward, but it is not without its challenges. As a doorknocker, you'll encounter a wide range of people, opinions, and situations—some welcoming and others less so. Knowing how to handle these challenges effectively is crucial to maintaining your composure, staying on message, and ensuring your safety. These skills will not only make you a more effective doorknocker but will also help you navigate the complexities of voter engagement with confidence and poise.

## Overcoming Objections and Resistance

One of the most common challenges you'll face as a doorknocker is overcoming objections and resistance from voters. Whether they are skeptical about your candidate, disillusioned with the political process, or simply resistant to engaging in conversation, it's important to approach these situations with empathy, understanding, and a well-prepared strategy.

### 1. Understanding the Nature of Objections

Objections from voters can take many forms, from mild skepticism to outright opposition. Understanding the underlying reasons for these objections is the first step in addressing them effectively. Some common types of objections you may encounter include:

- **Policy Disagreements:** Voters may object to specific policies or positions held by your candidate. They may have strong opinions about issues such as taxes, healthcare, education, or immigration, and may express these disagreements during your conversation.

- **Distrust of Politicians:** Some voters may express a general distrust of politicians, believing that they are all corrupt, self-serving, or disconnected from the needs of ordinary people. This type of objection is often rooted in frustration with the political system as a whole.

- **Apathy and Disinterest:** A significant number of voters may be apathetic or disinterested in politics altogether. They may feel that their vote doesn't matter or that no candidate truly represents their interests.

- **Personal Experiences:** Voters may object based on personal experiences that have shaped their views. For example, someone who has had a negative experience with government bureaucracy might be skeptical of any candidate's promises to improve the system.

- **Partisan Loyalty:** Some voters may be loyal to another party or candidate and object to your message simply because they view it as conflicting with their political identity.

## 2. Strategies for Overcoming Objections

Overcoming objections requires a combination of empathy, knowledge, and persuasive communication. Here are some strategies for addressing different types of objections:

- **Listen Actively:** The first step in overcoming an objection is to listen actively to what the voter is saying. This means not interrupting, giving them your full attention, and showing that you genuinely care about their concerns. Active listening helps build rapport and demonstrates that you respect their opinions, even if you disagree.

- **Acknowledge Their Concerns:** Before responding to an objection, it's important to acknowledge the voter's concerns. This can be as simple as saying, "I understand why you feel that way," or "I can see why that's important to you." Acknowledging their concerns helps to validate their feelings and makes them more receptive to your response.

- **Provide Information:** Once you've acknowledged the voter's concerns, provide clear and concise information that addresses their objections. Focus on facts, evidence, and specific examples that support your candidate's position. For example, if a voter objects to your candidate's healthcare policy, you might provide details about how the policy will benefit people in their community.

- **Find Common Ground:** Look for areas of agreement or shared values that you can build on. For example, even if a voter disagrees with your candidate's approach to taxes, you might find common ground on the importance of funding public services like education and healthcare. Finding common ground helps to create a more collaborative and less adversarial conversation.

- **Use Stories and Personal Examples:** Stories and personal examples can be powerful tools for overcoming objections. Sharing a story about how your candidate's policies have helped real people can make your message more relatable and compelling. For example, you might share a story about a family who benefited from a similar policy in another community.

- **Stay Respectful and Non-Confrontational:** It's important to remain respectful and non-confrontational, even if the voter is expressing strong objections. Avoid getting defensive or argumentative, and instead, focus on calmly presenting your case. Remember that your goal is not to "win" the argument but to build understanding and trust.

- **Offer to Follow Up:** If a voter's objections are complex or if they request more information, offer to follow up with additional details. This could involve sending them campaign literature, directing them to the candidate's website, or arranging for someone from the campaign to contact them with more information. Offering to follow up shows that you are committed to addressing their concerns and are willing to go the extra mile.

### 3. Example Scenarios for Overcoming Objections

Let's explore a few example scenarios where you might encounter objections and how you can effectively address them:

**Scenario 1: Policy Disagreement on Taxes**

Voter: "I don't agree with your candidate's plan to raise taxes. I'm already paying too much, and I don't see why I should pay more."

Response: "I understand that taxes are a concern for many people, and it's important that they're used wisely. Our candidate's plan is focused on ensuring that those who can afford it pay their fair share, so we can invest in critical services like education, healthcare, and infrastructure. These investments will benefit everyone in our community, and there are measures in place to protect middle-class families from paying more."

## Scenario 2: Distrust of Politicians

Voter: "Politicians always make promises, but they never keep them. Why should I believe that your candidate is any different?"

Response: "I completely understand your frustration. It's true that people have been let down by politicians in the past. What I can tell you about our candidate is that they have a proven track record of delivering on their promises. For example, in their last role, they successfully passed legislation that improved local schools and expanded healthcare access. They're running because they genuinely care about making a difference, and they're committed to being accountable to the people they serve."

## Scenario 3: Apathy and Disinterest

Voter: "I don't really follow politics. I don't think my vote makes a difference anyway."

Response: "It's easy to feel that way, especially with everything going on. But your vote really does matter, especially in close races like this one. The decisions made by our elected leaders have a direct impact on our daily lives—from the quality of our schools to the safety of our streets. Our candidate is focused on making sure that everyone's voice is heard and that the government works for all of us, not just the powerful. I'd love to share more about how they plan to do that."

## Managing Tough Questions and Staying on Message

As a doorknocker, you will inevitably encounter tough questions from voters—questions that challenge your candidate's positions, address controversial issues, or require you to clarify complex policies. Handling these questions effectively is essential to maintaining credibility, staying on message, and fostering constructive dialogue.

## 1. Types of Tough Questions

Tough questions can come in many forms, including:

- **Policy-Specific Questions:** These questions may focus on specific aspects of your candidate's platform, such as their stance on healthcare, immigration, or economic policy. Voters may seek detailed explanations or challenge the feasibility of certain proposals.

- **Controversial or Sensitive Issues:** Voters may ask about controversial or sensitive issues, such as racial justice,

LGBTQ+ rights, or gun control. These topics can be emotionally charged, and it's important to address them with care and sensitivity.

- **Character and Integrity:** Questions about your candidate's character, integrity, or past actions can be particularly challenging, especially if they involve accusations or criticisms.

- **Comparisons with Opponents:** Voters may ask you to compare your candidate with their opponents, highlighting perceived weaknesses or differences. These questions can put you on the spot and require careful navigation.

## 2. Strategies for Managing Tough Questions

When faced with tough questions, it's important to stay composed, confident, and on message. Here are some strategies for effectively managing tough questions:

- **Prepare Thoroughly:** The best way to handle tough questions is to be well-prepared. Familiarize yourself with your candidate's platform, policies, and positions on key issues. Practice answering common questions and anticipate potential challenges. The more prepared you are, the more confident and credible you will be when faced with tough questions.

- **Stay On Message:** It's important to stay on message and keep the focus on your candidate's key priorities and values. Even when answering a challenging question, try to steer the conversation back to the main points you want to emphasize. For example, if a voter questions a specific policy, you might acknowledge their concern and then highlight how the policy aligns with the candidate's broader vision for the community.

- **Be Honest and Transparent:** If you don't know the answer to a question, it's better to be honest than to guess or provide incorrect information. You might say, "That's a great question, and I want to make sure I give you the correct information. I'll look into it and get back to you with more details." Honesty and transparency help build trust and credibility with voters.

- **Address the Question Directly:** When faced with a tough question, it's important to address it directly rather than deflecting or avoiding it. Acknowledging the voter's concern and providing a thoughtful response demonstrates that you take their question seriously and are willing to engage in meaningful dialogue.

- **Keep Your Cool:** Tough questions can sometimes be provocative or confrontational. It's important to remain calm, composed, and respectful, even if the voter's tone is challenging. Responding with patience and professionalism helps defuse tension and keeps the conversation constructive.

- **Use Bridging Statements:** Bridging statements are a useful tool for steering the conversation back to your main message. For example, if a voter asks a tough question about a controversial issue, you might respond with, "That's an important concern, and it's something our candidate has thought a lot about. What they're really focused on is [key message]." This allows you to acknowledge the question while also emphasizing the broader goals of the campaign.

- **Know When to Redirect:** In some cases, a voter's question may be outside the scope of your knowledge or may require a more detailed response than you can provide on the spot. In these situations, it's okay to redirect the voter to additional resources, such as the campaign's website, or offer to have someone from the campaign follow up with them.

## 3. Example Scenarios for Managing Tough Questions

Let's explore a few example scenarios where you might encounter tough questions and how you can effectively manage them:

### Scenario 1: Policy-Specific Question on Immigration

Voter: "I'm concerned about your candidate's stance on immigration. How will they address the issue of illegal immigration without harming those who are already here?"

Response: "That's a very important question, and it's something our candidate takes very seriously. Their approach to immigration is focused on finding a fair and humane solution that balances security with compassion. They support comprehensive immigration reform that includes a pathway to citizenship for those who are already here, while also strengthening border security and ensuring that our immigration system is fair and efficient. The goal is to create a system that reflects our values as a nation and treats everyone with dignity."

### Scenario 2: Controversial Issue on Gun Control

Voter: "I'm a gun owner, and I'm worried about your candidate's position on gun control. Are they going to try to take away my guns?"

Response: "I understand your concerns, and I want to reassure you that our candidate fully supports the Second Amendment and the rights of responsible gun owners. Their focus is on implementing common-sense measures to reduce gun violence and keep our communities safe, such as background checks and closing loopholes that allow dangerous individuals to access firearms. These measures are about protecting public safety while respecting the rights of law-abiding citizens."

## Scenario 3: Character Question on Past Actions

Voter: "I've heard some negative things about your candidate's past. How can I trust that they're the right person for the job?"

Response: "I appreciate your concern, and I think it's important to look at the full picture of who our candidate is and what they stand for. Like all of us, they've faced challenges and made mistakes in the past, but what's really important is how they've learned from those experiences and how they're using that knowledge to serve our community. Our candidate has a strong record of public service, and they're committed to being a leader we can trust. I'd be happy to share more about their accomplishments and vision for the future."

## Dealing with Negative or Confrontational Situations

While most voters you encounter will be polite and respectful, there may be times when you face negative or confrontational situations. Whether it's a voter who is openly hostile, someone who interrupts or challenges you aggressively, or an encounter that feels threatening, it's important to know how to handle these situations with grace and professionalism.

## 1. Recognizing and Defusing Tension

The first step in dealing with a negative or confrontational situation is recognizing the signs of tension and taking steps to defuse it. Some common signs of tension include raised voices, crossed arms, aggressive body language, or dismissive comments. Here are some strategies for defusing tension:

- **Stay Calm and Composed:** Your own demeanor can have a significant impact on the tone of the conversation. By staying calm, composed, and speaking in a steady, even tone, you can help de-escalate the situation and prevent it from escalating further.

- **Acknowledge Emotions:** If the voter is visibly upset or angry, it's important to acknowledge their emotions without taking them personally. You might say, "I can see that this issue is really important to you, and I appreciate you sharing your perspective." Acknowledging their emotions can help them feel heard and may reduce their frustration.

- **Use De-Escalation Techniques:** De-escalation techniques, such as active listening, empathizing, and finding common ground, can help calm a tense situation. For example, you might say, "I understand where you're coming from, and I think we both want what's best for our community. Let's talk about how we can find a solution that works for everyone."

- **Avoid Reacting to Provocation:** In some cases, a voter may try to provoke you by making inflammatory or confrontational statements. It's important not to take the bait. Instead, stay focused on your message and avoid getting drawn into an argument.

## 2. Managing Aggressive or Hostile Behavior

If a voter's behavior becomes aggressive or hostile, it's important to prioritize your safety and well-being. Here are some tips for managing aggressive or hostile behavior:

- **Know When to Walk Away:** If a voter becomes verbally abusive, threatens you, or refuses to engage in a constructive conversation, it's okay to politely end the interaction and walk away. You might say, "I'm sorry we couldn't find common ground today. I appreciate your time, and I hope you have a good day." Then, calmly leave the situation.

- **Stay Alert and Aware:** Always be aware of your surroundings and trust your instincts. If something doesn't feel right or if you sense that a situation could become dangerous, remove yourself from the area and seek a safe place.

- **Keep a Safe Distance:** If a voter becomes physically aggressive or invades your personal space, it's important to maintain a safe distance. Step back and position yourself so that you have a clear path to exit the situation if necessary.

- **Report the Incident:** If you experience a serious or threatening situation, report the incident to your campaign supervisor or local authorities as appropriate. Provide as much detail as possible, including the location, description of the individual, and any relevant circumstances.

## 3. Example Scenarios for Dealing with Negative or Confrontational Situations

Let's explore a few example scenarios where you might encounter negative or confrontational situations and how you can effectively manage them:

### Scenario 1: Hostile Voter on the Opposing Candidate

Voter: "Your candidate is a fraud, and I can't believe you're out here supporting them! You people are ruining this country!"

Response: "I can see that you feel very strongly about this, and I respect your right to have your own opinions. My goal here today is to have a constructive conversation and to share why I believe our candidate is the right choice for our community. If you're interested, I'd be happy to discuss some of the issues that are important to you."

If the voter continues to be hostile: "I understand that we may not agree on everything, and that's okay. Thank you for your time, and I hope you have a good day."

### Scenario 2: Aggressive Behavior

Voter: (Aggressively) "Why don't you just get off my property? I don't want to hear anything you have to say!"

Response: "I'm sorry to have disturbed you. I'll leave right away. Thank you for your time."

If the situation feels unsafe: Calmly leave the property and report the incident to your campaign supervisor. Prioritize your safety and do not engage further.

**Scenario 3: Negative Comments on Social Media**

Voter: "I'm going to post about this on social media. People need to know how terrible your candidate is!"

Response: "You're absolutely free to share your views, and I respect that. I would just ask that you consider all the facts and the positive impact our candidate has had on the community before making a final judgment. If you'd like more information, I'm happy to provide it."

If the voter is determined to post negatively: "I appreciate your time today, and I hope you'll take the time to learn more about our candidate before the election."

**Staying Safe in Unfriendly or Unpredictable Environments**

While most doorknocking experiences are positive, there may be times when you find yourself in unfriendly or unpredictable environments. Your safety should always be your top priority, and it's important to take proactive steps to protect yourself while engaging with voters.

**1. Assessing the Environment**

Before you begin doorknocking in a new area, take the time to assess the environment and identify any potential risks. Here are some factors to consider:

- **Neighborhood Reputation:** Research the neighborhood's reputation to understand any safety concerns, such as high crime rates, gang activity, or recent incidents of violence. If an area has a history of safety issues, consider whether it's appropriate to canvass there or whether additional precautions are needed.

- **Time of Day:** The time of day can have a significant impact on your safety. It's generally safer to doorknock during daylight hours when there is more activity and visibility. Avoid canvassing after dark or in isolated areas where there are fewer people around.

- **Accessibility and Visibility:** Consider the layout of the neighborhood, including the visibility of houses from the street and the accessibility of entrances. Be cautious when approaching homes with poor visibility, tall fences, or secluded locations.

- **Local Knowledge:** If possible, seek input from local residents or campaign team members who are familiar with the area. They can provide valuable insights into any specific safety concerns and offer advice on how to navigate the neighborhood.

## 2. Safety Tips for Doorknocking

Here are some general safety tips to keep in mind while doorknocking:

- **Doorknock in Pairs:** Whenever possible, doorknock with a partner. Having a second person with you provides an extra layer of safety and support. If one person feels uncomfortable or threatened, the other can help de-escalate the situation or call for assistance.

- **Keep Your Phone Handy:** Always carry your phone with you and keep it easily accessible. Ensure that your phone is fully charged before you start doorknocking and that you have important contacts, such as your campaign supervisor or emergency services, saved in your phone. Keep a backup battery on hand as well.

- **Trust Your Instincts:** If something doesn't feel right or if you feel uncomfortable in a particular situation, trust your instincts and remove yourself from the area. It's better to err on the side of caution than to put yourself in a potentially dangerous situation.

- **Avoid Entering Homes:** As a general rule, avoid entering a voter's home, even if they invite you inside. Politely decline by saying something like, "Thank you for the offer, but I'm not allowed to enter homes while canvassing." If you do need to enter a building, such as an apartment complex, ensure that you feel comfortable and that the area is well-lit and secure.

- **Be Mindful of Personal Information:** Avoid sharing personal information with voters, such as your home address, phone number, or social media profiles. Keep the focus on the campaign and the issues at hand, and maintain a professional boundary.

- **Have an Exit Plan:** Before you approach a door, have an exit plan in mind. Identify the quickest route back to the street or to a safer area, and be prepared to leave quickly if necessary.

- **Stay Visible:** If you're doorknocking alone, try to stay in areas with high visibility and where other people are present. Avoid isolated areas or homes that are set far back from the road.

- **Stay Alert:** Do not let your guard down. Be mindful of your surroundings. Know your exit points and anything that can be used as an improvised weapon if the voter gets violent. This is rare, but be prepared.

## 3. Example Scenarios for Staying Safe

Let's explore a few example scenarios where safety may be a concern and how you can effectively protect yourself:

### Scenario 1: Unfriendly Neighborhood

You arrive in a neighborhood where there are signs of neglect, and you notice groups of people loitering in the streets, some of whom are staring at you as you walk by.

Response: Trust your instincts and consider whether it's safe to continue doorknocking in this area. If you feel uncomfortable or unsafe, it's okay to leave the neighborhood and report your concerns to your campaign supervisor. They may decide to avoid the area or send a team of canvassers to increase safety.

### Scenario 2: Approaching a Secluded Home

You approach a home that is set far back from the road, surrounded by tall trees, and with no other houses in sight.

Response: Consider the risks of approaching a secluded home. If you feel uncomfortable, it may be safer to skip this house and move on to the next one. Alternatively, if you're doorknocking with a partner, discuss your concerns with them and decide whether it's safe to proceed together.

## Scenario 3: Encountering an Aggressive Dog

You approach a home, and as you get closer, a large dog starts barking aggressively and charging toward you.

Response: Stop immediately and assess the situation. If the dog is not restrained or if you feel threatened, back away slowly and calmly, avoiding sudden movements. Do not turn your back on the dog, and if necessary, use a barrier (such as a clipboard) to protect yourself. If the situation feels too risky, skip this house and move on to the next one. Some people may tell you to keep dog treats in your pocket to give to dogs, and while this sounds like excellent advice, you do not know the dietary restrictions or allergies of any dogs you may encounter. A good way to make sure a voter never votes for the party/candidate you represent is to kill their pet. This would also create extremely negative publicity.

## Navigating Challenges with Confidence

Handling common challenges is an essential skill for any doorknocker, and it's what separates effective canvassers from those who struggle. By learning how to overcome objections, manage tough questions, deal with negative or confrontational situations, and stay safe in unfriendly environments, you can approach your doorknocking efforts with confidence and resilience.

Remember that every challenge you encounter is an opportunity to learn and grow as a canvasser. With practice and preparation, you can develop the skills needed to navigate difficult situations, build stronger connections with voters, and contribute to the success of your campaign.

As you continue your doorknocking journey, keep these strategies in mind and don't hesitate to seek support from your campaign team when needed. You are not alone in this effort, and together, you can overcome any challenge that comes your way.

# 6: Assembling Your Doorknocking Kit

Doorknocking is a physically demanding and mentally engaging activity that requires careful preparation. To ensure that your efforts are successful and that you are prepared for any situation that might arise, it's essential to assemble a comprehensive doorknocking kit. Whether you're a seasoned campaigner or a first-time volunteer, having the right kit can make all the difference in your effectiveness and comfort as you engage with voters.

## Essential Items to Carry

When preparing for a day of doorknocking, it's important to carry a variety of essential items that will help you stay safe, comfortable, and effective. These items are the foundation of your doorknocking kit and should be included every time you head out.

## 1. First Aid Kit

Accidents and minor injuries can happen during a long day of doorknocking, especially when you're covering a lot of ground. A basic first aid kit is an essential part of your kit, ensuring that you're prepared to handle minor cuts, scrapes, blisters, or other common issues.

What to Include in Your First Aid Kit:

- **Band-Aids:** Carry a variety of sizes to cover minor cuts and blisters.

- **Antiseptic Wipes:** Use these to clean cuts or scrapes before applying a bandage.

- **Gauze Pads and Medical Tape:** These are useful for covering larger wounds or for creating makeshift bandages.

- **Blister Pads or Moleskin:** If you're walking long distances, blisters can become a problem. Blister pads or moleskin can help prevent or treat blisters.

- **Pain Relievers:** Carry over-the-counter pain relievers like ibuprofen or acetaminophen to help with headaches, muscle aches, or other minor pains.

- **Tweezers:** Useful for removing splinters or ticks if you're doorknocking in wooded or rural areas.

- **Hydrocortisone Cream:** This can help alleviate itching from bug bites or minor skin irritations.

## 2. Extra Shoe Laces

Shoe laces might not seem like an obvious item to carry, but they can be a lifesaver if one of your laces breaks during a long day of doorknocking. Broken laces can slow you down and make it uncomfortable to walk, so having an extra pair in your kit ensures that you won't be sidelined by such a small issue.

Why Extra Shoe Laces Are Important:

- **Durability:** If you're walking a lot, your laces can wear down and break unexpectedly.

- **Comfort:** A broken lace can make your shoe fit poorly, leading to discomfort or blisters.

- **Versatility:** In a pinch, shoe laces can also be used as a makeshift tie or strap for securing other items.

### 3. Water and Snacks

Staying hydrated and energized is crucial during a day of doorknocking. You'll be on your feet for hours, and it's easy to get dehydrated or fatigued if you don't take care of your basic needs. Carrying water and snacks ensures that you can keep going strong throughout the day.

What to Include:

- **Water Bottle:** A reusable water bottle is a must. Consider one with insulation to keep your water cool, especially on hot days. Refill it whenever you have the chance.

- **Electrolyte Packets:** These can be added to your water to help replace lost electrolytes, which is especially important if you're sweating a lot.

- **Energy Bars or Snacks:** Choose snacks that are easy to carry and provide sustained energy, such as granola bars, trail mix, or fruit. Avoid snacks that are messy or perishable.

- **Fruits:** Apples, bananas, or oranges are great for quick energy and hydration.

### 4. Phone Charger and Power Bank

Your phone is one of your most important tools during doorknocking. You'll use it for navigation, communication, and possibly logging voter interactions. To ensure that your phone doesn't run out of juice, always carry a charger and a portable power bank.

Why You Need a Phone Charger and Power Bank:

- **Staying Connected:** Your phone keeps you connected to your campaign team and allows you to call for help if needed.

- **Navigation:** Use your phone for GPS and mapping tools to ensure you're following your planned route.

- **Voter Data:** If you're using a canvassing app, your phone will likely be running the app throughout the day, which can drain the battery quickly.

- **Backup Power:** A power bank allows you to recharge your phone on the go, even if you don't have access to an outlet.

## Clothing Essentials

What you wear while doorknocking can have a significant impact on your comfort, safety, and effectiveness. It's important to choose clothing that is appropriate for the weather, the terrain, and the duration of your canvassing.

### 1. Comfortable Shoes

The most important piece of clothing for any doorknocker is a comfortable pair of shoes. You'll be on your feet for hours, walking long distances, and possibly navigating uneven terrain, so your shoes need to provide support, cushioning, and durability.

What to Look for in Doorknocking Shoes:

- **Support:** Choose shoes that offer good arch support and cushioning to prevent foot fatigue and reduce the risk of injury.

- **Durability:** Your shoes should be durable enough to withstand long days of walking, including on sidewalks, grass, gravel, and dirt paths.

- **Breathability:** Shoes that allow your feet to breathe will help prevent overheating and reduce the risk of blisters.

- **Water Resistance:** If you're doorknocking in wet conditions, water-resistant shoes can help keep your feet dry and comfortable.

## 2. Weather-Appropriate Attire

The weather can vary greatly during the campaign season, and it's important to dress appropriately to stay comfortable and safe. Here's how to prepare for different weather conditions:

- **Hot Weather:** Wear lightweight, breathable clothing that wicks away sweat. Consider a wide-brimmed hat or a cap to protect your face from the sun. Don't forget sunglasses and sunscreen to protect your skin and eyes.

- **Cold Weather:** Layering is key in cold weather. Start with a moisture-wicking base layer to keep sweat away from your skin, add an insulating layer for warmth, and finish with a windproof and waterproof outer layer to protect against the elements. A warm hat, gloves, and a scarf are also essential.

- **Rainy Weather:** A lightweight, waterproof jacket with a hood is a must for rainy days. Consider waterproof pants and shoes to keep yourself dry. An umbrella can also be useful, but make sure it's sturdy enough to withstand wind.

- **Windy Weather:** On windy days, wear clothing that blocks the wind, such as a windbreaker or a jacket with a windproof layer. Secure loose clothing, hats, or papers to prevent them from being blown away.

## 3. Change of Clothes

A change of clothes is always a good idea, especially if you're doorknocking in variable weather conditions or if you're spending the entire day canvassing. Having a fresh set of clothes can make a big difference in your comfort and confidence.

When to Bring a Change of Clothes:

- **Unpredictable Weather:** If there's a chance of rain, mud, or drastic temperature changes, a change of clothes ensures you can stay dry and comfortable.

- **Long Days:** After several hours of walking, you might appreciate changing into fresh clothes before continuing your canvassing or heading to an event.

- **Spills and Accidents**: Accidents happen, whether it's spilling food or drink, getting caught in the rain, or stepping in a puddle. A change of clothes helps you stay presentable.

## Safety Gear

Your safety is the top priority while doorknocking. Depending on the area you're canvassing and the conditions, you may need to carry specific safety gear to protect yourself.

## 1. Bulletproof Vest

In some high-risk areas, particularly where there have been threats of violence or where tensions are high, wearing a bulletproof vest may be a necessary precaution. This is a personal decision and should be based on an assessment of the risks involved.

When to Consider a Bulletproof Vest:

- **High-Risk Areas:** If you're canvassing in areas with a history of violence or where there are credible threats, a bulletproof vest can provide an added layer of protection.

- **Special Events:** During protests, large gatherings, or other events where emotions may run high, a bulletproof vest might be recommended.

- **Guidance from Campaign Leaders:** Follow the advice of your campaign leaders regarding the necessity of a bulletproof vest. They will have the best information on the risks associated with specific areas.

## 2. Whistle

A whistle is a simple but effective tool for attracting attention in an emergency. If you feel threatened or need help, blowing a whistle can alert others nearby and potentially deter an attacker.

Why a Whistle Is Important:

- **Emergency Alert:** A loud whistle can be heard from a distance, making it an effective way to signal for help if you're in danger.

- **Deterrent:** The noise of a whistle can startle and deter someone who might be considering an attack.

- **Compact and Lightweight:** A whistle is small, lightweight, and easy to carry on a lanyard or attached to your bag.

## 3. Pepper Spray

Pepper spray is another personal safety tool that can be used to defend yourself in case of an attack. It's a non-lethal option that can incapacitate an assailant long enough for you to escape and seek help.

When to Carry Pepper Spray:

- **Personal Safety:** If you're canvassing in an area where you feel there's a risk of physical confrontation, carrying pepper spray can give you added peace of mind.

- **Legal Considerations:** Be aware of the laws regarding pepper spray in your area. In some places, there may be restrictions on carrying or using pepper spray, so make sure you're informed and compliant with local regulations.

- **Training:** If you choose to carry pepper spray, it's important to know how to use it properly. Practice using it in a safe environment so that you're prepared to deploy it quickly and effectively if needed.

## Useful Tools

In addition to safety gear and essentials for your comfort, you'll need a variety of tools to help you carry out your doorknocking duties effectively. These tools will ensure that you have everything you need to engage with voters, gather information, and stay organized.

### 1. Maps and Navigation Tools

Knowing where you're going is crucial for effective doorknocking. Whether you're using digital maps or paper maps, make sure you have the tools you need to navigate your route.

Digital Navigation Tools:

- **GPS Apps:** Use GPS apps like Google Maps, Apple Maps, or Waze to plan your route and navigate to specific addresses. These apps can provide real-time directions and traffic updates.

- **Canvassing Apps:** If your campaign uses a canvassing app, it may include built-in mapping and navigation features that help you follow your route and track the houses you've visited.

- **Battery Backup:** As mentioned earlier, always carry a charger and power bank to ensure your phone stays powered throughout the day.

- **Printed Maps:** If you prefer to use paper maps, print out maps of your target area and highlight your planned route. This can be a helpful backup in case your phone dies or you lose signal.

- **Map Book:** Consider carrying a small map book that covers the entire area you'll be canvassing. This can be especially useful in rural or less-developed areas where digital maps might not be as accurate.

## 2. Flyers and Campaign Literature

Flyers and campaign literature are essential tools for doorknocking. They provide voters with information about your candidate and their platform and give them something tangible to remember the conversation.

What to Include in Your Campaign Literature:

- **Candidate Information:** Include a brief bio of the candidate, their key positions on important issues, and any relevant experience or accomplishments.

- **Key Messages:** Highlight the main points you want voters to remember, such as the candidate's vision, priorities, and what sets them apart from their opponents.

- **Contact Information:** Provide contact details for the campaign, including the website, social media handles, and phone number. This makes it easy for voters to get more information or get involved.

- **Event Invitations:** If there are upcoming campaign events, include invitations or information about how voters can attend.

## 3. Pens and Notepads

You'll need pens and notepads to take notes during your doorknocking. Whether you're jotting down voter information, recording feedback, or making a note of someone who wants to be contacted later, having a reliable way to write things down is essential.

Why Pens and Notepads Are Important:

- **Recording Voter Interactions:** Keep track of who you've spoken to, what issues they're concerned about, and any follow-up actions that are needed.

- **Taking Notes:** Use your notepad to jot down important information, such as voter names, phone numbers, or specific questions that you need to research further.

- **Backup for Digital Tools:** If your phone dies or if you prefer to take notes by hand, a pen and notepad serve as a reliable backup.

## 4. Voter Information Sheets

Voter information sheets are helpful for tracking your interactions with voters and ensuring that you have all the necessary information to follow up later. These sheets can be customized based on your campaign's needs and can include a variety of fields.

What to Include on Voter Information Sheets:

- **Voter Name and Address:** Record the voter's name and address to keep track of who you've spoken to.

- **Party Affiliation:** Note the voter's party affiliation if known. This can help guide your conversation and determine the likelihood of support.

- **Support Level:** Use a scale to indicate how supportive the voter is of your candidate, ranging from strong support to undecided to opposition.

- **Key Issues:** Record the issues that are most important to the voter, such as healthcare, education, or the economy.

- **Follow-Up Needed:** Make a note of any follow-up actions that are needed, such as sending more information, scheduling a call, or inviting the voter to an event.

- **Additional Comments:** Include a space for any additional comments or observations that could be helpful for the campaign.

## How to Pack Efficiently and Keep Your Kit Organized

Having all the necessary items for doorknocking is important, but it's equally important to pack efficiently and keep your kit organized. This ensures that you can find what you need quickly and that you're not weighed down by unnecessary items.

### 1. Choosing the Right Bag

The first step in packing efficiently is choosing the right bag to carry your items. Your bag should be comfortable, durable, and have enough compartments to keep everything organized.

Types of Bags to Consider:

- **Backpack:** A backpack is a great option for doorknocking because it distributes weight evenly across your shoulders and back, reducing strain. Look for a backpack with multiple compartments and padding for comfort.

- **Messenger Bag:** A messenger bag can be a good option if you prefer something smaller and easier to access quickly. However, be mindful of the weight distribution, as carrying a heavy messenger bag on one shoulder can become uncomfortable over time.

- **Tote Bag:** A tote bag is a simple option that allows for easy access to your items. However, it may not be the best choice if you're carrying a lot of heavy items or if you need to walk long distances.

- **Fanny Pack or Waist Bag:** If you prefer to carry only the essentials and want something lightweight, a fanny pack or waist bag can be a good choice. It's great for holding your phone, keys, and a few small items.

## 2. Packing Essentials and Organizing Your Bag

Once you've chosen your bag, it's time to pack your items efficiently. Here are some tips for organizing your bag:

- **Use Compartments:** Take advantage of your bag's compartments to keep items organized and easy to find. For example, use one compartment for your first aid kit, another for snacks and water, and a separate compartment for pens, notepads, and voter information sheets.

- **Pack Heavy Items at the Bottom:** Place heavier items, such as your water bottle and power bank, at the bottom of your bag. This helps distribute weight evenly and makes it easier to carry.

- **Keep Frequently Used Items Accessible:** Items that you'll use frequently, such as your phone, pens, and campaign literature, should be packed in easily accessible compartments. This way, you don't have to dig through your bag every time you need something.

- **Roll, Don't Fold:** When packing extra clothes, roll them instead of folding. Rolling saves space and reduces wrinkles, making it easier to fit everything in your bag.

- **Use Small Pouches:** Consider using small pouches or organizers for smaller items like pens, chargers, and first aid supplies. This helps prevent items from getting lost in the bottom of your bag and makes it easier to find what you need quickly.

- **Stay Organized Throughout the Day:** As you go through your day of doorknocking, make an effort to stay organized. Put items back in their designated compartments after using them, and take a few moments to reorganize your bag if it starts to get messy.

## 3. Keeping Your Bag Lightweight

While it's important to carry all the necessary items, it's equally important to avoid overpacking and making your bag too heavy. A heavy bag can become uncomfortable and exhausting to carry, especially after several hours of walking.

Tips for Keeping Your Bag Lightweight:

- **Prioritize Essentials:** Focus on packing only the items that you know you'll need. Leave behind anything that isn't essential for the day.

- **Use Multi-Functional Items:** Choose items that serve multiple purposes. For example, a multi-tool can replace several individual tools, and a scarf can be used for warmth, sun protection, or as a makeshift bag.

- **Decant Liquids:** If you're carrying liquids like sunscreen or hand sanitizer, consider transferring them into smaller travel-sized bottles to save space and reduce weight.

- **Reevaluate Regularly:** Periodically review the items in your bag and remove anything that you haven't used or no longer need. This helps prevent your bag from becoming cluttered with unnecessary items.

### The Well-Prepared Doorknocker

Assembling a well-organized and efficient doorknocking kit is key to a successful day of canvassing. By carefully selecting the essential items, clothing, safety gear, and tools you'll need, and by packing them in a way that keeps everything accessible and lightweight, you'll be ready to tackle the challenges of doorknocking with confidence.

Remember, the goal of your kit is to keep you safe, comfortable, and effective as you engage with voters. Take the time to prepare thoroughly, and you'll be able to focus on what really matters—connecting with voters, sharing your candidate's message, and making a positive impact on your community.

With your doorknocking kit ready to go, you'll be equipped to handle whatever the day throws at you, from changing weather conditions to unexpected challenges. Stay organized, stay prepared, and most importantly, stay committed to your mission of making a difference, one door at a time.

# Chapter 7: Safety and Self-Care on the Trail

Doorknocking is one of the most demanding and rewarding activities in a political campaign, but it also comes with its own set of risks and challenges. Spending long hours in unfamiliar neighborhoods, dealing with a variety of people, and constantly being on the move can take a toll on both your physical and mental well-being.

**Recognizing and Mitigating Risks in the Field**

When you're out doorknocking, your safety is paramount. Recognizing potential risks and knowing how to mitigate them is crucial for avoiding dangerous situations and ensuring that you can focus on your mission without unnecessary worry. In this section, we'll discuss how to identify different types of risks and what steps you can take to reduce them.

**1. Assessing Neighborhood Safety**

The first step in mitigating risks is to assess the safety of the neighborhood where you'll be doorknocking. While most neighborhoods are safe, some areas may present more challenges, particularly if they have a history of crime or other safety concerns. Here's how to assess neighborhood safety:

- **Research the Area:** Before you head out, take some time to research the neighborhood. Look up crime statistics, local news reports, and community reviews to get a sense of the area's safety. Websites like NeighborhoodScout or local police department reports can provide valuable insights.

- **Consult with Local Residents:** If possible, talk to people who live or work in the area to get their perspective on the neighborhood. They can provide firsthand information about any potential risks and may offer advice on which areas to avoid.

- **Check with the Campaign:** Your campaign team should have information about the areas you'll be canvassing, including any known safety concerns. Make sure to consult with your campaign leaders before heading out, especially if you're unfamiliar with the area.

- **Observe the Environment:** When you arrive in the neighborhood, take a moment to observe your surroundings. Look for signs of neglect, such as broken windows, graffiti, or poorly lit streets, which might indicate a higher risk of crime. Pay attention to the presence of security measures, like neighborhood watch signs or security cameras, which can indicate either a proactive community or a response to past issues.

## 2. Identifying Specific Risks

In addition to assessing the overall safety of a neighborhood, it's important to be aware of specific risks that you might encounter while doorknocking. These risks can vary depending on the area, time of day, and other factors.

Common Risks to Consider:

- **Aggressive Animals:** Some neighborhoods may have loose or aggressive dogs that could pose a threat. Be cautious when approaching homes with "Beware of Dog" signs or when you hear barking behind a fence or door.

- **Unfriendly or Hostile Residents:** While most people are polite, you may encounter residents who are unfriendly, confrontational, or even hostile. This is particularly true in politically polarized areas where tensions may run high.

- **Environmental Hazards:** Weather conditions, uneven terrain, and poorly maintained sidewalks can all pose risks. Slips, trips, and falls are common hazards, especially in areas with steep hills, icy sidewalks, or loose gravel.

- **Traffic and Road Safety:** If you're doorknocking in a busy area with lots of traffic, be mindful of the risk of accidents. Crossing busy streets, navigating narrow sidewalks, or working near construction zones can all increase your risk of injury.

### 3. Mitigating Risks: Practical Strategies

Once you've identified potential risks, the next step is to take proactive measures to mitigate them. Here are some practical strategies to keep yourself safe:

- **Work in Pairs:** Whenever possible, doorknock with a partner. This provides an extra layer of safety, as you can watch out for each other, offer assistance if needed, and deter potential threats by not being alone.

- **Carry Safety Gear:** As discussed in Chapter 6, carrying safety gear like a whistle, pepper spray, and a charged phone can help you stay safe in case of an emergency. Make sure your safety gear is easily accessible and that you know how to use it.

- **Set Check-In Times:** Establish regular check-in times with your campaign team or a trusted contact. Let them know your location and your planned route, and check in periodically to confirm that you're safe. This ensures that someone knows where you are at all times.

- **Avoid Isolated Areas:** Stick to well-traveled streets and avoid isolated areas, especially after dark. If you're doorknocking in a rural area, be cautious about approaching homes that are set far back from the road or surrounded by dense vegetation.

- **Trust Your Instincts:** If something doesn't feel right, trust your instincts and leave the area. It's better to skip a few houses than to put yourself in a potentially dangerous situation.

## Techniques for Staying Alert and Aware of Your Surroundings

Staying alert and aware of your surroundings is one of the most important aspects of staying safe while doorknocking. By maintaining situational awareness, you can identify potential threats before they become problems and react quickly to any changes in your environment. Here are some techniques for staying alert and aware:

### 1. The Importance of Situational Awareness

Situational awareness is the ability to perceive and understand what is happening around you and to anticipate how these events might affect you. It involves constantly monitoring your environment, assessing potential risks, and being prepared to take action if necessary.

Why Situational Awareness Is Critical:

- **Prevention:** Being aware of your surroundings helps you avoid dangerous situations before they escalate. For example, noticing a group of people acting suspiciously might prompt you to change your route.

- **Response:** If a threat does arise, situational awareness allows you to respond more quickly and effectively. Whether it's crossing the street to avoid a confrontation or calling for help, being alert helps you take the right action at the right time.

- **Confidence:** Maintaining situational awareness can also boost your confidence, as you'll feel more in control of your environment and better prepared to handle whatever comes your way.

## 2. Techniques for Maintaining Situational Awareness

Maintaining situational awareness while doorknocking requires focus and mindfulness. Here are some techniques to help you stay alert:

- **Keep Your Head Up:** Avoid walking with your head down or staring at your phone. Keep your head up, your eyes scanning the environment, and your posture confident. This not only helps you stay aware but also makes you appear more assertive and less likely to be targeted.

- **Use All Your Senses:** Situational awareness isn't just about what you see—it's also about what you hear and feel. Pay attention to sounds, such as approaching footsteps, car engines, or barking dogs. Notice changes in the weather or temperature, which could signal a storm or other environmental hazards.

- **Take Mental Snapshots:** As you move through a neighborhood, take mental snapshots of your surroundings. Note landmarks, such as street signs, large trees, or distinctive buildings, which can help you orient yourself and recognize if something changes.

- **Be Mindful of Blind Spots:** Be cautious when approaching corners, doorways, or other areas where your view is obstructed. Slow down and check for any potential hazards before proceeding. This is especially important when walking past driveways, where cars may be backing out.

- **Limit Distractions:** While it's important to stay connected with your campaign team, try to limit distractions while you're doorknocking. Avoid using headphones, as they can make it difficult to hear what's happening around you. If you need to check your phone or take notes, do so briefly and then return to scanning your environment.

- **Practice the "OODA Loop":** The OODA Loop (Observe, Orient, Decide, Act) is a decision-making process used by military and law enforcement personnel to maintain situational awareness. It involves constantly observing your surroundings, orienting yourself to any changes, deciding on a course of action, and then acting. By practicing this process, you can stay alert and respond quickly to any potential threats.

## 3. Recognizing Signs of Trouble

Part of staying aware of your surroundings is recognizing the signs of potential trouble before it escalates. Here are some warning signs to watch out for:

- **Unusual Behavior:** Pay attention to people who are acting strangely or out of place. This could include someone loitering in a residential area, someone watching you from a distance, or someone approaching you in an aggressive manner.

- **Crowded or Chaotic Environments:** Large crowds or chaotic environments can be disorienting and increase the risk of accidents or confrontations. Be cautious when navigating through busy areas, and be prepared to leave if the situation feels unsafe.

- **Blocked Exits or Pathways:** If you notice that an exit or pathway is blocked, either by people, vehicles, or obstacles, be cautious. This could be a sign of trouble, or it could limit your ability to leave the area quickly if needed.

- **Intimidating Groups:** If you encounter a group of people who appear to be intimidating or hostile, consider avoiding them or changing your route. Groups can be more difficult to manage than individuals, and it's better to avoid a potential confrontation.

**Physical and Mental Self-Care Tips: Staying Hydrated, Taking Breaks, and Managing Stress**

Doorknocking is physically and mentally demanding work. To ensure that you can sustain your efforts over the course of a campaign, it's important to prioritize self-care. This includes staying hydrated, taking regular breaks, managing stress, and listening to your body's needs.

## 1. The Importance of Staying Hydrated

Staying hydrated is essential for maintaining your energy levels, focus, and overall well-being while doorknocking. Dehydration can lead to fatigue, headaches, dizziness, and impaired decision-making, all of which can affect your performance and safety.

Tips for Staying Hydrated:

- **Carry a Water Bottle:** Always carry a reusable water bottle with you, and take sips regularly throughout the day. Choose a bottle with insulation to keep your water cool, especially on hot days.

- **Monitor Your Hydration Levels:** Pay attention to signs of dehydration, such as dry mouth, dark urine, or feeling lightheaded. If you notice these symptoms, increase your water intake and take a break in a cool, shaded area.

- **Drink Before You're Thirsty:** Don't wait until you're thirsty to drink water. Thirst is a late sign of dehydration, so aim to drink small amounts of water consistently throughout the day.

- **Avoid Dehydrating Beverages:** Beverages like coffee, soda, and alcohol can contribute to dehydration, so it's best to limit their consumption while doorknocking. Stick to water, or consider adding an electrolyte supplement to your water to help maintain your hydration levels.

## 2. Taking Regular Breaks

Taking regular breaks is important for preventing physical and mental fatigue. When you're focused on reaching as many voters as possible, it can be tempting to push through without stopping, but this can lead to burnout and decreased effectiveness.

How to Incorporate Breaks:

- **Plan Your Breaks:** Before you start your day, plan regular breaks into your schedule. Aim to take a short break every hour or two, depending on your pace and the conditions. Use this time to rest, stretch, and hydrate.

- **Find a Comfortable Spot:** When it's time for a break, find a comfortable spot to sit down and relax. Look for a park bench, a shady tree, or a quiet café where you can take a few minutes to recharge.

- **Listen to Your Body:** Pay attention to how your body feels. If you start to feel fatigued, sore, or lightheaded, take a break even if it's not part of your planned schedule. It's better to take a few minutes to recover than to push yourself too hard and risk injury or exhaustion.

- **Use Breaks to Check-In:** Use your breaks as an opportunity to check in with your campaign team, review your progress, and adjust your plan if needed. This can help you stay on track and maintain your motivation throughout the day.

## 3. Managing Stress and Mental Health

Doorknocking can be mentally and emotionally challenging, especially if you encounter difficult voters, face rejection, or experience long days with little rest. Managing stress and taking care of your mental health is crucial for maintaining your resilience and staying focused on your goals.

Strategies for Managing Stress:

- **Practice Deep Breathing:** Deep breathing is a simple but effective way to manage stress in the moment. If you start to feel overwhelmed, take a few slow, deep breaths, inhaling through your nose and exhaling through your mouth. This can help calm your nervous system and reduce feelings of anxiety.

- **Stay Positive:** Focus on the positive aspects of your work and remind yourself of the impact you're making. Celebrate small victories, such as a successful conversation with a voter, and use these moments to stay motivated.

- **Practice Mindfulness:** Mindfulness involves staying present in the moment and observing your thoughts and feelings without judgment. If you find yourself ruminating on a negative experience or worrying about the future, try to bring your attention back to the present moment. This can help reduce stress and improve your mental clarity.

- **Set Realistic Expectations:** It's important to set realistic expectations for yourself and your work. Not every interaction will go perfectly, and that's okay. Focus on doing your best and remember that every effort counts, even if you don't see immediate results.

- **Seek Support:** Don't hesitate to reach out for support if you're feeling stressed or overwhelmed. Talk to your campaign team, a trusted friend, or a mental health professional if needed. Sharing your feelings and getting advice from others can help you navigate challenging situations and maintain your mental well-being.

## How to Recognize Signs of Burnout and How to Address It

Burnout is a state of physical, emotional, and mental exhaustion caused by prolonged stress and overwork. It's a common issue in high-pressure environments like political campaigns, where the demands of the job can be intense and relentless. Recognizing the signs of burnout and taking steps to address it is essential for your long-term health and effectiveness.

### 1. Recognizing the Signs of Burnout

Burnout doesn't happen overnight—it's a gradual process that builds up over time. Here are some common signs of burnout to watch out for:

- **Physical Symptoms:** Persistent fatigue, headaches, muscle tension, and changes in sleep patterns are all common physical symptoms of burnout. You might also experience a weakened immune system, leading to frequent illnesses.

- **Emotional Symptoms:** Burnout can cause feelings of frustration, irritability, anxiety, and a sense of being overwhelmed. You might also experience a loss of motivation or enthusiasm for your work.

- **Cognitive Symptoms:** Difficulty concentrating, memory problems, and a sense of mental fogginess are all cognitive symptoms of burnout. You might find it harder to make decisions or stay focused on tasks.

- **Behavioral Symptoms:** Burnout can lead to changes in behavior, such as withdrawing from social interactions, avoiding responsibilities, or becoming more cynical or negative. You might also notice that you're procrastinating more or struggling to complete tasks.

- **Performance Decline:** As burnout progresses, you might notice a decline in your performance, both in terms of quantity and quality. You might struggle to meet deadlines, make more mistakes, or feel less satisfied with your work.

## 2. Addressing Burnout: Prevention and Recovery

Preventing and recovering from burnout requires a combination of self-care, boundary-setting, and seeking support. Here's how to address burnout if you start to notice the signs:

- **Prioritize Self-Care:** Make self-care a priority in your daily routine. This includes getting enough sleep, eating nutritious meals, staying hydrated, and engaging in regular physical activity. Self-care also involves taking time for activities that you enjoy and that help you relax, such as reading, spending time in nature, or practicing a hobby.

- **Set Boundaries:** It's important to set boundaries around your work to prevent burnout. This might involve limiting the number of hours you spend doorknocking each day, saying no to additional responsibilities, or scheduling regular time off. Setting boundaries helps protect your energy and ensures that you have time to rest and recharge.

- **Take Time Off:** If you're feeling burned out, taking time off can be an important step in your recovery. Whether it's a day off to relax or a longer break to recharge, time away from work can help you regain your energy and perspective. Use this time to focus on self-care and to engage in activities that bring you joy.

- **Seek Support:** Don't try to manage burnout on your own—seek support from others. Talk to your campaign team about how you're feeling and discuss any adjustments that can be made to your workload. Reach out to friends, family, or a therapist for emotional support and guidance.

- **Reevaluate Your Goals:** Take some time to reflect on your goals and priorities. If you're feeling burned out, it might be helpful to reassess your goals and make any necessary adjustments. This could involve setting more realistic expectations, focusing on the aspects of your work that bring you the most satisfaction, or finding new ways to contribute to the campaign.

## Staying Safe and Healthy on the Trail

Doorknocking is a demanding but incredibly rewarding activity that plays a crucial role in the success of a political campaign. By prioritizing your safety and self-care, you can ensure that you're able to sustain your efforts over the long haul and make a meaningful impact.

Remember that your well-being is just as important as the work you're doing. Take the time to recognize potential risks, stay alert and aware of your surroundings, and practice self-care strategies that keep you physically and mentally healthy. If you start to notice signs of burnout, don't hesitate to take action and seek support.

As you continue your doorknocking journey, keep these strategies in mind and make self-care an integral part of your routine. By taking care of yourself, you'll be better equipped to take care of the voters you're engaging with and to contribute to the success of your candidate and campaign.

# Chapter 8: Engaging in Meaningful Conversations

Engaging in meaningful conversations with voters is the heart of doorknocking. It's the moment when you connect directly with individuals, share your candidate's vision, and, most importantly, listen to their concerns and needs. Building rapport quickly, demonstrating empathy, navigating sensitive topics, and leaving a positive lasting impression are all crucial skills that can make the difference between a voter feeling heard and valued, or simply another door knocked on.

## Building Rapport with Voters Quickly

Building rapport is about establishing a connection with voters in a short amount of time. You may only have a few minutes—or even seconds—to make an impression, so it's essential to use this time wisely. Rapport creates a sense of trust and mutual respect, making voters more receptive to your message.

## 1. Start with a Friendly Introduction

First impressions are critical, and the way you introduce yourself sets the tone for the entire interaction. A friendly, polite, and confident introduction can help put voters at ease and make them more open to conversation.

Steps for a Strong Introduction:

- **Smile and Make Eye Contact:** A genuine smile and direct eye contact convey warmth, confidence, and sincerity. These non-verbal cues are powerful in making voters feel comfortable and respected.

- **State Your Name and Affiliation:** Clearly state your name and that you're a volunteer or representative for [Candidate's Name]'s campaign. For example, "Hi, my name is [Your Name], and I'm a volunteer with [Candidate's Name]. I'm out here today to talk with folks about the upcoming election."

- **Acknowledge Their Time:** Respecting the voter's time is crucial. You might say something like, "I appreciate you taking a moment to chat with me today." This shows that you're considerate of their schedule and won't take up too much of their time.

- **Express Enthusiasm:** Show enthusiasm for your role and for the candidate you're representing. Voters are more likely to engage with someone who is passionate and genuinely believes in the cause.

## 2. Find Common Ground

Finding common ground is a key component of building rapport. It allows you to connect with voters on a personal level, making the conversation feel less like a sales pitch and more like a friendly discussion.

How to Find Common Ground:

- **Ask Open-Ended Questions:** Open-ended questions encourage voters to share more about themselves and their views. For example, "What issues are most important to you in this election?" or "How do you feel about the direction our community is heading?" These questions invite the voter to express their thoughts and give you insight into their priorities.

- **Listen for Cues:** Pay attention to any clues the voter might give about their interests or concerns. For example, if you notice a bumper sticker, lawn sign, or any other indicator of their values or affiliations, use that as a starting point for discussion.

- **Share Personal Stories:** Sharing a brief personal story can help humanize the conversation and create a bond. For example, "I'm passionate about this campaign because I have kids in the local school system, and I want to ensure they get the best education possible."

- **Agree on Shared Values:** Even if you don't agree on everything, there are often shared values or goals that you can highlight. For example, "I think we both want what's best for our community, even if we have different ideas on how to get there."

## 3. Be Genuine and Authentic

Voters can tell when someone is being insincere. Being genuine and authentic in your interactions is crucial for building trust and rapport.

Tips for Authenticity:

- **Be Yourself:** Don't try to adopt a persona that isn't true to who you are. Authenticity comes across in your tone, body language, and choice of words.

- **Speak from the Heart:** Share your genuine reasons for supporting the candidate or cause. Personal conviction is compelling and can resonate with voters on a deeper level.

- **Avoid Scripted Responses:** While it's important to be prepared, avoid sounding like you're reading from a script. Engage in a real conversation and adapt your message based on the voter's responses.

**The Importance of Empathy and Active Listening**

Empathy and active listening are perhaps the most powerful tools in your doorknocking toolkit. They enable you to truly understand the voter's perspective, demonstrate that you care about their concerns, and build a stronger connection.

**1. What Is Empathy in the Context of Doorknocking?**

Empathy is the ability to understand and share the feelings of another person. In the context of doorknocking, empathy means putting yourself in the voter's shoes, recognizing their emotions and concerns, and responding in a way that shows you genuinely care.

Why Empathy Matters:

- **Builds Trust:** When voters feel that you understand and care about their concerns, they are more likely to trust you and your candidate.

- **Fosters Connection:** Empathy creates a sense of connection and rapport, making voters more receptive to your message.

- **Improves Communication:** Understanding the voter's perspective allows you to tailor your message in a way that resonates with them and addresses their specific needs.

## 2. Practicing Active Listening

Active listening is a key component of empathy. It involves fully focusing on the voter, understanding their message, and responding thoughtfully. Active listening goes beyond just hearing the words they say; it's about understanding the underlying emotions and concerns.

Techniques for Active Listening:

- **Give Your Full Attention:** Focus entirely on the voter when they're speaking. Avoid distractions, such as checking your phone or looking around the neighborhood. Show that you're fully engaged in the conversation.

- **Use Non-Verbal Cues:** Nod your head, maintain eye contact, and use facial expressions that show you're following along and understanding their points. These non-verbal cues reinforce that you're actively listening.

- **Paraphrase and Reflect:** After the voter has spoken, paraphrase what they've said to confirm your understanding. For example, "It sounds like you're really concerned about the cost of healthcare. Is that right?" This shows that you're not only listening but also processing their message.

- **Ask Clarifying Questions:** If you're not sure what the voter means, ask clarifying questions to get more information. For example, "Can you tell me more about your experience with that issue?" or "What do you think would be the best solution?"

- **Respond Thoughtfully:** When it's your turn to speak, respond in a way that acknowledges the voter's concerns and connects them to your candidate's platform. For example, "I understand that healthcare costs are a big issue for you. Our candidate has a plan to address that by [specific policy]."

### 3. Empathy in Action: Real-World Scenarios

Here are some examples of how you can apply empathy and active listening in different doorknocking scenarios:

### Scenario 1: A Voter Expresses Frustration with the Political System

Voter: "I'm fed up with politicians. They make promises, but nothing ever changes. Why should I trust your candidate?"

Response: "I completely understand your frustration. It can be really disheartening when it feels like the system isn't working for us. One of the things I admire about [Candidate's Name] is that they've consistently worked to keep their promises. For example, they've [specific accomplishment], which has made a real difference for people in our community. I think they're different because they genuinely listen to people like you."

### Scenario 2: A Voter Is Concerned About the Impact of a Specific Policy

Voter: "I'm worried that [policy] will hurt small businesses like mine. What's your candidate going to do about that?"

Response: "Thank you for sharing that concern—I know how important small businesses are to our community. [Candidate's Name] has a plan that takes into account the needs of small business owners. They're committed to ensuring that any new policies provide support and resources to help businesses like yours thrive. I'd love to share more about the specific measures they're proposing."

## Scenario 3: A Voter Is Skeptical About Change

Voter: "I've heard it all before—candidates talk about change, but everything stays the same."

Response: "I can see why you feel that way, especially if you've been disappointed in the past. What I find encouraging about [Candidate's Name] is that they've already demonstrated their ability to make positive changes, even when it's tough. For instance, they [specific example of change they've made]. I believe they're the right person to bring about the change we need."

## Navigating Difficult or Sensitive Topics Without Alienating Voters

Political conversations can often touch on difficult or sensitive topics. Whether it's a deeply personal issue, a polarizing policy, or a controversial stance, it's important to navigate these conversations carefully to avoid alienating voters.

## 1. Recognizing Sensitive Topics

Sensitive topics can vary widely depending on the voter's background, values, and experiences. Some common sensitive topics in political conversations include:

- **Social Issues:** Topics like abortion, LGBTQ+ rights, racial justice, and immigration can be deeply personal and emotionally charged.

- **Economic Policies**: Discussions about taxes, welfare, and healthcare often involve strong opinions and can impact voters' livelihoods directly.

- **National Security:** Issues related to national security, military intervention, and foreign policy can evoke strong patriotic or moral beliefs.

- **Personal Experiences:** Voters may have personal experiences that influence their views on certain issues, such as losing a job, dealing with illness, or experiencing discrimination.

## 2. Approaching Sensitive Topics with Care

When approaching sensitive topics, it's crucial to do so with empathy, respect, and a focus on finding common ground. Here's how to handle these conversations:

- **Acknowledge the Sensitivity:** Start by acknowledging that the topic is sensitive and that you respect the voter's perspective. For example, "I know this is a deeply personal issue for many people, and I want to approach it with the respect it deserves."

- **Listen Before Responding:** Allow the voter to express their views fully before responding. Listening first shows that you're open to understanding their perspective and aren't just waiting to present your own argument.

- **Avoid Confrontation:** If the voter has a strong opinion that differs from your candidate's stance, avoid turning the conversation into a confrontation. Instead, focus on understanding their concerns and finding points of agreement where possible.

- **Share Your Candidate's Position Thoughtfully:** When presenting your candidate's position on a sensitive issue, do so in a way that acknowledges the complexity of the topic. For example, "Our candidate understands that this is a complex issue with no easy answers. They've taken a thoughtful approach by [specific policy details] and are committed to finding a solution that respects everyone's rights and values."

- **Respect Differences:** If it becomes clear that you and the voter have fundamentally different views on a sensitive issue, respect those differences. You might say, "I can see that we have different perspectives on this, and I respect your right to hold those views. What I appreciate about [Candidate's Name] is that they're committed to representing all of us, even when we don't agree on every issue."

## 3. Diffusing Tension in Difficult Conversations

Sometimes, discussions on sensitive topics can become tense or heated. It's important to know how to diffuse tension and keep the conversation constructive.

Techniques for Diffusing Tension:

- **Stay Calm and Composed:** If the conversation starts to become heated, stay calm and composed. Lower your voice slightly, speak slowly, and avoid interrupting the voter.

- **Acknowledge Emotions:** If the voter is visibly upset or angry, acknowledge their emotions without dismissing them. For example, "I can see that this issue is really important to you, and I respect that."

- **Redirect the Conversation:** If the conversation is becoming too confrontational, try to redirect it to a less contentious topic. For example, "I understand that we have strong feelings about this issue. I'd love to hear your thoughts on [another issue]."

- **End on a Positive Note:** If you feel that the conversation isn't going anywhere productive, it's okay to end it on a positive note. For example, "I appreciate you taking the time to share your views with me. I'll take what you've said back to the campaign. Thank you for your time today."

## Tips for Leaving a Positive Lasting Impression

The end of the conversation is just as important as the beginning. How you conclude your interaction can leave a lasting impression that influences the voter's perception of your candidate and campaign. Here's how to ensure that you leave a positive, memorable impression:

### 1. Summarize Key Points

Before wrapping up the conversation, briefly summarize the key points you've discussed. This reinforces your message and ensures that the voter leaves with a clear understanding of your candidate's position.

How to Summarize Effectively:

- **Highlight Shared Values:** Emphasize any common ground you've found during the conversation. For example, "It's great that we both care about making our community a better place. [Candidate's Name] is committed to doing just that by [key policy points]."

- **Reiterate the Candidate's Vision:** Remind the voter of your candidate's overall vision and goals. For example, "At the end of the day, [Candidate's Name] is focused on creating opportunities for everyone in our community. That's why they're running for office."

- **Address Any Remaining Concerns:** If the voter has expressed concerns during the conversation, acknowledge them again and offer reassurance. For example, "I know you had some concerns about [issue], and I'll make sure the campaign knows about it. Your feedback is really valuable."

## 2. Provide Campaign Materials

Leaving the voter with campaign materials gives them something to remember your conversation by and provides them with additional information to review later.

What to Include in Campaign Materials:

- **Candidate's Biography and Platform:** Include a brief bio of the candidate and an overview of their key platform points.

- **Contact Information:** Provide contact details for the campaign, including a website, phone number, and social media handles. This makes it easy for the voter to reach out if they have further questions.

- **Upcoming Events:** If there are any upcoming campaign events, include information about how the voter can attend or get involved.

- **Voter Information:** Provide details about voting locations, dates, and how to register if the voter isn't already registered.

## 3. Express Gratitude

Always end the conversation by thanking the voter for their time. This shows that you appreciate their willingness to engage, regardless of whether they agree with your candidate's views.

Examples of Expressing Gratitude:

- "Thank you so much for taking the time to talk with me today. I really appreciate your insights."

- "I'm grateful for your time and your willingness to discuss these important issues. It's been a pleasure speaking with you."

- "Thanks again for your time. Your feedback is valuable, and I'll make sure to share it with the campaign."

## 4. Offer to Follow Up

If the voter expressed interest in learning more or had questions that you couldn't fully address during the conversation, offer to follow up with additional information.

How to Offer Follow-Up:

- "I'll make sure to pass along your questions to the campaign team, and we'll get back to you with more information."

- "If you'd like, I can send you more details about [specific policy] or connect you with someone from the campaign who can answer your questions."

- "Feel free to reach out to us if you have any more questions or thoughts. We're here to help and to listen."

## 5. Leave a Positive Note for Absentees

If the voter isn't home, consider leaving a personalized note along with the campaign materials. This can create a positive impression, even if you didn't get to speak with them directly.

What to Include in the Note:

- **Introduce Yourself and the Campaign:** Briefly introduce yourself and mention that you stopped by on behalf of [Candidate's Name].

- **Express Your Enthusiasm:** Share a sentence or two about why you're excited about the campaign and why you believe the voter might be interested.

- **Encourage Follow-Up:** Encourage the voter to reach out if they have any questions or if they'd like to learn more about the campaign.

## The Power of Meaningful Conversations

Engaging in meaningful conversations with voters is the cornerstone of successful doorknocking. By building rapport quickly, practicing empathy and active listening, navigating sensitive topics with care, and leaving a positive lasting impression, you can make a significant impact on the voter's perception of your candidate and campaign.

Remember that every interaction, no matter how brief, is an opportunity to connect with someone and to share your passion for the issues and values that matter to you. By approaching each conversation with sincerity, respect, and a commitment to understanding the voter's perspective, you can help build the trust and support that are essential for winning hearts, minds, and ultimately, votes.

As you continue your doorknocking efforts, keep these strategies in mind and use them to create meaningful, impactful conversations that leave a lasting positive impression on every voter you meet.

# Chapter 9: Working with a Team

While doorknocking often involves individual effort, it's essential to recognize that you are part of a larger team working towards a common goal. Whether you're canvassing with a partner, a small group, or coordinating with campaign headquarters, teamwork plays a crucial role in the success of any political campaign. Understanding how to work effectively with others, communicate well, and handle conflicts when they arise can make your canvassing efforts more efficient, enjoyable, and impactful.

## The Benefits of Canvassing with a Partner or Group

While canvassing solo can be an effective way to cover ground and engage with voters, there are significant benefits to working with a partner or as part of a group. These benefits include increased safety, enhanced motivation, and the ability to leverage different strengths and perspectives.

### 1. Increased Safety

One of the primary benefits of canvassing with a partner or group is the increased safety it provides. Canvassing involves interacting with strangers, navigating unfamiliar neighborhoods, and spending long hours on the move. Having a partner or group with you can reduce risks and provide a sense of security.

Safety Benefits of Team Canvassing:

- **Deterrence of Potential Threats:** Individuals are less likely to encounter hostility or aggression when they are with others. A team presence can act as a deterrent to potential threats, making it less likely that you'll face unsafe situations.

- **Assistance in Emergencies:** If you or your partner encounter a medical emergency or any other crisis, having another person there to assist, call for help, or provide first aid is invaluable.

- **Enhanced Situational Awareness:** With multiple people on the lookout, you can cover more ground and remain aware of your surroundings more effectively. Your partner or group members might notice potential hazards that you could miss on your own.

- **Support in Navigating Difficult Conversations:** If a conversation with a voter becomes challenging or confrontational, having a partner can help you navigate the situation more smoothly. Your partner can step in to help defuse tension, offer a different perspective, or simply provide moral support.

## 2. Enhanced Motivation and Morale

Canvassing, while rewarding, can be exhausting work. Long hours, rejection, and the physical demands of the job can take a toll on your motivation and morale. Working with a partner or group can help keep spirits high and make the experience more enjoyable.

How Team Canvassing Boosts Morale:

- **Mutual Encouragement:** When you're working with others, you can encourage each other to keep going, even when you're feeling tired or discouraged. A simple "We're doing great!" from a partner can make a big difference in your energy levels and motivation.

- **Shared Accomplishments:** Celebrating small victories together, such as a successful conversation with a voter or reaching a canvassing milestone, can create a sense of camaraderie and shared purpose.

- **Social Interaction:** Canvassing with a partner or group provides opportunities for social interaction, which can make the day more enjoyable and help break up the monotony of long hours spent knocking on doors. Chatting between houses, sharing stories, and even a bit of friendly competition can make the experience more fun.

- **Team Accountability:** When you're part of a team, there's a natural sense of accountability. Knowing that others are counting on you to show up and do your part can help you stay committed, even when the work gets tough.

### 3. Leveraging Different Strengths and Perspectives

Every team member brings their own unique strengths, experiences, and perspectives to the table. By working together, you can leverage these differences to enhance your canvassing efforts and reach a broader range of voters.

**Benefits of Diverse Team Dynamics:**

- **Complementary Skills:** One team member might be particularly skilled at engaging with older voters, while another excels at connecting with younger or more diverse demographics. By pairing up, you can cover a wider range of voters more effectively.

- **Varied Perspectives:** Different team members may bring different perspectives to discussions, allowing you to approach conversations with voters more thoughtfully and inclusively. This can be especially valuable when navigating complex or sensitive topics.

- **Shared Problem-Solving:** When faced with a challenge, such as a difficult voter or an unexpected logistical issue, having multiple minds working together can lead to more creative and effective solutions.

- **Learning Opportunities:** Working with others provides opportunities to learn from each other's experiences and approaches. By observing your partner or group members, you can pick up new strategies, refine your techniques, and become a more effective canvasser.

## Coordinating with Campaign Headquarters for Support and Updates

Effective coordination with campaign headquarters is essential for ensuring that your canvassing efforts are aligned with the overall strategy and that you have the support and resources you need to succeed. This section will explore how to coordinate effectively with headquarters, stay updated on important developments, and make the most of the support available to you.

## 1. Understanding the Role of Campaign Headquarters

Campaign headquarters serves as the nerve center of the campaign. It's where strategies are developed, data is analyzed, and resources are allocated. For canvassers, headquarters is a critical source of information, guidance, and support.

Key Functions of Campaign Headquarters:

- **Strategy and Messaging:** Headquarters develops the overall strategy for the campaign, including key messaging, voter targeting, and priorities. They provide canvassers with the talking points and materials needed to stay on message and effectively engage with voters.

- **Data Management:** Headquarters collects and analyzes data from canvassing efforts, such as voter responses, turnout trends, and demographic information. This data helps refine the campaign's strategy and ensures that resources are allocated efficiently.

- **Resource Allocation:** Headquarters is responsible for distributing resources, such as campaign literature, signs, and supplies, to canvassing teams. They also manage logistical support, such as transportation, volunteer coordination, and communication tools.

- **Training and Support:** Headquarters provides training for canvassers, ensuring that everyone is well-prepared to represent the campaign. They also offer ongoing support, such as answering questions, resolving issues, and providing updates on campaign developments.

## 2. Staying Updated on Campaign Developments

Campaigns are dynamic and fast-paced, with strategies and priorities that can shift quickly in response to new information or changing circumstances. Staying updated on campaign developments is crucial for ensuring that your canvassing efforts are aligned with the current goals and messaging.

Ways to Stay Informed:

- **Regular Briefings:** Attend regular briefings or check-ins organized by the campaign headquarters. These meetings provide updates on the campaign's progress, changes in strategy, and any new information that canvassers need to know.

- **Communication Channels:** Make sure you're connected to the campaign's communication channels, such as email lists, group chats, or messaging apps. These channels are often used to share important updates, reminders, and instructions.

- **Daily Updates:** Some campaigns provide daily updates to canvassers, either through emails or a dedicated app. These updates might include information about the day's priorities, talking points, or any new issues that have arisen.

- **Access to Resources:** Familiarize yourself with the campaign's online resources, such as websites, intranets, or shared drives. These platforms often house key documents, training materials, and other resources that can help you stay informed and prepared.

- **Direct Communication with HQ:** If you have questions or need clarification on any aspect of the campaign, don't hesitate to reach out directly to headquarters. Whether it's through a phone call, email, or a messaging app, staying in close contact with HQ ensures that you're always in the loop.

## 3. Utilizing Support from Headquarters

Campaign headquarters is there to support you, and it's important to make the most of the resources and assistance they provide. Whether you need more materials, have a logistical question, or encounter an issue in the field, headquarters can help ensure that your canvassing efforts run smoothly.

How to Access Support from HQ:

- **Requesting Materials:** If you're running low on campaign literature, signs, or other materials, contact headquarters to request more. They can arrange for supplies to be delivered or provide instructions on where to pick them up.

- **Seeking Guidance:** If you encounter a difficult situation, such as a confrontational voter or a question you can't answer, reach out to headquarters for guidance. They can provide advice on how to handle the situation or direct you to the appropriate resources.

- **Reporting Issues:** If you encounter any logistical issues, such as problems with your route, difficulties accessing certain areas, or safety concerns, report them to headquarters as soon as possible. They can help resolve the issue or adjust your plans accordingly.

- **Providing Feedback:** Don't hesitate to share your experiences and observations with headquarters. Whether it's feedback on voter responses, suggestions for improving the canvassing process, or insights into local issues, your input can help refine the campaign's strategy and make future canvassing efforts more effective.

## Communicating Effectively with Your Team: Sharing Information and Feedback

Effective communication within your canvassing team is essential for ensuring that everyone is on the same page, working towards common goals, and able to support one another. Whether you're sharing information, providing feedback, or coordinating efforts, clear and open communication is key to a successful team dynamic.

## 1. The Importance of Open Communication

Open communication is the foundation of effective teamwork. It ensures that everyone has the information they need to do their job, helps prevent misunderstandings, and fosters a positive team environment.

Why Open Communication Matters:

- **Ensures Consistency:** By sharing information openly, you ensure that all team members are consistent in their messaging and approach. This consistency is crucial for maintaining the credibility and effectiveness of the campaign.

- Facilitates Collaboration: Open communication encourages collaboration and allows team members to share ideas, solve problems together, and support one another in their efforts.

- **Builds Trust:** When team members communicate openly and honestly, it builds trust within the team. Trust is essential for creating a positive and productive working environment.

- **Improves Efficiency:** Clear communication helps prevent misunderstandings and reduces the need for repeated explanations or corrections. This improves the overall efficiency of the team's efforts.

## 2. Sharing Information Effectively

Sharing information effectively within your team involves ensuring that everyone has access to the same data, updates, and resources. It also means communicating in a way that is clear, concise, and easy to understand.

**Tips for Sharing Information:**

- **Use Centralized Platforms:** If your team is using digital tools for communication, make sure that all relevant information is shared through a centralized platform, such as a group chat, messaging app, or shared drive. This ensures that everyone has access to the same information.

- **Be Clear and Concise:** When sharing information, be clear and concise. Avoid jargon or overly complex language, and make sure your message is easy to understand. If you're providing instructions, break them down into simple, actionable steps.

- **Confirm Receipt:** After sharing important information, confirm that all team members have received and understood it. This can be as simple as asking for a thumbs-up in a group chat or checking in with team members individually.

- **Provide Context:** When sharing updates or new information, provide context to help your team understand why the information is important and how it impacts their work. For example, if you're sharing a change in strategy, explain the reasoning behind the change and how it will affect your canvassing efforts.

## 3. Providing Constructive Feedback

Providing feedback is an important part of working in a team, but it's essential to do so in a way that is constructive and supportive. Constructive feedback helps team members improve their performance, learn new skills, and feel valued for their contributions.

How to Give Constructive Feedback:

- **Focus on Specific Behaviors:** When providing feedback, focus on specific behaviors or actions rather than generalizations. For example, instead of saying, "You're not engaging with voters enough," you might say, "I noticed that in our last few conversations, you didn't ask as many open-ended questions. Maybe we could try incorporating more of those to encourage voters to share their thoughts."

- **Be Supportive:** Frame your feedback in a positive and supportive way. Acknowledge the team member's efforts and offer suggestions for improvement rather than simply pointing out what they did wrong. For example, "You're doing a great job of staying on message, and I think if we work on pacing, we can make our conversations even more impactful."

- **Use "I" Statements:** Using "I" statements can help you express your feedback in a non-confrontational way. For example, "I felt that the voter responded well when we focused on local issues. Maybe we could emphasize those more in our conversations."

- **Encourage Open Dialogue:** Encourage team members to ask questions or share their thoughts in response to your feedback. This fosters a collaborative environment where everyone feels comfortable discussing their experiences and learning from one another.

## 4. Receiving Feedback Graciously

Just as it's important to give feedback constructively, it's equally important to receive feedback graciously. Being open to feedback from your team members helps you grow as a canvasser and contributes to a positive team dynamic.

Tips for Receiving Feedback:

- **Listen Actively:** When receiving feedback, listen actively and give the speaker your full attention. Avoid interrupting or getting defensive, and focus on understanding their perspective.

- **Ask Clarifying Questions:** If you're not sure what the feedback means or how to implement it, ask clarifying questions. For example, "Can you give me an example of how I could improve in that area?"

- **Express Gratitude:** Thank the person for their feedback, even if it's difficult to hear. A simple "Thank you for sharing that with me" shows that you appreciate their input and are willing to learn from it.

- **Reflect and Apply:** Take time to reflect on the feedback and consider how you can apply it to your canvassing efforts. If the feedback is actionable, make a plan for how you'll incorporate it into your work.

## Handling Conflicts or Disagreements Within the Team

Even the most cohesive teams can experience conflicts or disagreements from time to time. How these conflicts are handled can significantly impact the team's morale, effectiveness, and overall success. In this section, we'll explore strategies for addressing conflicts constructively and maintaining a positive team dynamic.

### 1. Recognizing the Sources of Conflict

Conflicts within a team can arise from a variety of sources, including differences in personality, communication styles, goals, or approaches to the work. Recognizing the underlying causes of conflict is the first step in addressing it effectively.

Common Sources of Conflict:

- **Communication Breakdowns:** Misunderstandings or miscommunications can lead to frustration and conflict. For example, if instructions are unclear or if team members have different interpretations of a strategy, it can create confusion and tension.

- **Differing Work Styles:** Team members may have different approaches to their work, which can lead to conflicts if not managed effectively. For example, one person may prefer a fast-paced approach, while another may take a more methodical pace.

- **Conflicting Goals:** Conflicts can arise if team members have differing goals or priorities. For example, one team member may be focused on voter outreach, while another is more concerned with data collection, leading to disagreements about how to allocate time and resources.

- **Personality Clashes:** Differences in personality can sometimes lead to conflict, especially if team members have contrasting temperaments, communication styles, or ways of handling stress.

## 2. Strategies for Resolving Conflicts

Resolving conflicts within a team requires open communication, empathy, and a focus on finding mutually acceptable solutions. Here are some strategies for addressing conflicts constructively:

- **Approach the Situation Calmly:** When a conflict arises, it's important to approach the situation calmly and with a clear mind. Take a moment to breathe and collect your thoughts before engaging in a discussion. This helps prevent the situation from escalating and ensures that you can communicate effectively.

- **Use "I" Statements:** When discussing the conflict, use "I" statements to express your feelings and perspective without placing blame. For example, "I felt frustrated when we weren't able to stick to the plan because I think it's important for us to stay on track."

- **Seek to Understand the Other Person's Perspective:** Try to understand the other person's perspective and the reasons behind their actions or opinions. Ask open-ended questions and listen actively to their responses. For example, "Can you help me understand why you feel strongly about this approach?"

- **Focus on Finding Solutions:** Instead of dwelling on the problem, focus on finding a solution that works for everyone. Brainstorm together and consider different options. For example, "What if we tried a hybrid approach that incorporates both of our ideas?"

- **Agree on a Way Forward:** Once you've identified a solution, agree on a way forward and outline any specific actions that need to be taken. For example, "Let's agree to test this approach for the next week and then reassess based on the results."

- **Involve a Third Party if Needed:** If the conflict can't be resolved through direct communication, it may be helpful to involve a third party, such as a team leader or campaign coordinator, to mediate the discussion and help facilitate a resolution.

## 3. Preventing Future Conflicts

While conflicts are sometimes unavoidable, there are steps you can take to prevent them from occurring or to minimize their impact on the team.

Tips for Preventing Conflicts:

- **Set Clear Expectations**: Establish clear expectations for communication, work styles, and team dynamics from the outset. This helps prevent misunderstandings and ensures that everyone is on the same page.

- **Encourage Open Communication:** Foster a culture of open communication where team members feel comfortable sharing their thoughts, concerns, and feedback. Regular check-ins and discussions can help address issues before they escalate.

- **Acknowledge and Respect Differences:** Recognize that each team member brings their own unique strengths, experiences, and perspectives to the table. Acknowledge and respect these differences, and find ways to leverage them to enhance the team's effectiveness.

- **Address Issues Early:** If you notice tension or potential conflicts brewing, address them early before they escalate. A proactive approach can prevent small issues from becoming bigger problems.

**- Celebrate Successes Together:** Celebrating successes as a team helps build camaraderie and reinforces the sense of shared purpose. Whether it's a successful day of canvassing or reaching a campaign milestone, take time to acknowledge and celebrate your achievements together.

## The Power of Teamwork in Campaign Success

Working with a team is an integral part of any successful political campaign. By canvassing with a partner or group, coordinating effectively with campaign headquarters, communicating openly with your team, and resolving conflicts constructively, you can contribute to a positive and productive team dynamic that drives the campaign forward.

Remember that teamwork is about more than just dividing tasks—it's about supporting one another, leveraging each other's strengths, and working together towards a common goal. Whether you're in the field knocking on doors or collaborating with your team remotely, the relationships you build and the skills you develop will play a crucial role in the success of the campaign.

As you continue your canvassing efforts, keep these principles of teamwork in mind and strive to create a collaborative, supportive, and effective team environment. By doing so, you'll not only enhance your own effectiveness as a canvasser but also contribute to the overall success of the campaign and the positive impact it has on the community.

# Chapter 10: Dealing with Unexpected Situations

No matter how well-prepared you are, unexpected situations can arise while canvassing. From sudden medical emergencies to extreme weather conditions, hostile individuals, or encounters with law enforcement, it's essential to know how to handle these scenarios effectively. The key to navigating unexpected situations is to stay calm, think clearly, and adapt quickly to the changing circumstances.

## How to Handle Emergencies: From Medical Issues to Extreme Weather

Emergencies can occur at any time, and being prepared to respond appropriately is crucial. Whether you're dealing with a medical emergency, a natural disaster, or an unexpected weather event, knowing what to do can make all the difference in ensuring your safety and the safety of those around you.

### 1. Medical Emergencies

Medical emergencies can happen without warning, and knowing how to respond can save lives. Whether it's a minor injury or a life-threatening situation, the steps you take in the first few minutes are critical.

Common Medical Emergencies While Canvassing:

- **Heat Exhaustion and Heatstroke:** Prolonged exposure to high temperatures, especially when combined with physical activity, can lead to heat exhaustion or heatstroke. Symptoms include heavy sweating, weakness, dizziness, nausea, headache, and, in severe cases, confusion, fainting, or loss of consciousness.

- **Dehydration:** Dehydration occurs when the body loses more fluids than it takes in. Symptoms include dry mouth, thirst, dark urine, fatigue, dizziness, and confusion.

- **Injuries from Slips, Trips, and Falls:** Uneven sidewalks, wet surfaces, and other hazards can cause slips, trips, and falls, leading to sprains, fractures, or other injuries.

- **Heart Attack:** Although less common, a heart attack can occur, especially in individuals with pre-existing heart conditions. Symptoms include chest pain or discomfort, shortness of breath, nausea, and lightheadedness.

- **Allergic Reactions:** Allergic reactions can be triggered by insect stings, food, or environmental factors. Symptoms can range from mild (itching, hives) to severe (difficulty breathing, swelling of the face or throat).

Steps to Take in a Medical Emergency:

- **Assess the Situation:** Quickly assess the situation to determine the severity of the emergency. If the person is conscious and able to communicate, ask them how they feel and what happened. If they are unconscious or unresponsive, call for help immediately.

- **Call for Help:** If the situation is serious, call 911 or the local emergency number. Provide the dispatcher with as much information as possible, including your location, the nature of the emergency, and any symptoms the person is experiencing.

- **Administer First Aid:** If you're trained in first aid, provide assistance while waiting for emergency responders to arrive. For example, if someone is suffering from heat exhaustion, move them to a cooler place, give them water to drink, and cool their body with wet cloths. If they're unconscious, check their airway, breathing, and circulation, and perform CPR if necessary.

- **Stay Calm and Reassure the Person:** Keep the person calm and reassure them that help is on the way. Stay with them until medical professionals arrive and take over.

- **Document the Incident:** After the emergency is over, document what happened and report it to the campaign headquarters. This is important for record-keeping and for ensuring that any necessary follow-up is done.

## 2. Extreme Weather Conditions

Weather conditions can change rapidly, and canvassing in extreme weather can pose significant risks. Whether you're dealing with heatwaves, thunderstorms, heavy rain, or cold snaps, it's important to be prepared and know when to call it a day.

Common Extreme Weather Situations:

- **Heatwaves:** High temperatures can lead to heat-related illnesses such as heat exhaustion or heatstroke. Extended exposure to the sun can also cause sunburn and dehydration.

- **Thunderstorms:** Thunderstorms can bring heavy rain, lightning, strong winds, and even hail. Lightning strikes pose a serious risk, especially if you're in an open area.

- **Heavy Rain:** Heavy rain can cause flooding, slippery surfaces, and reduced visibility, making it dangerous to continue canvassing.

- **Cold Snaps and Snowstorms:** Cold weather can lead to frostbite, hypothermia, and dangerous road conditions. Snow and ice can also make walking treacherous.

Steps to Take in Extreme Weather:

- **Monitor Weather Reports:** Before heading out to canvass, check the weather forecast and stay informed about any severe weather warnings. If there's a significant risk, it's better to postpone canvassing until conditions improve.

- **Dress Appropriately:** Wear weather-appropriate clothing to protect yourself from the elements. In hot weather, wear light, breathable clothing and a wide-brimmed hat. In cold weather, layer your clothing, wear a warm hat, gloves, and insulated boots. In rainy weather, a waterproof jacket, pants, and boots are essential.

- **Take Regular Breaks:** In extreme heat or cold, take frequent breaks to rest and hydrate. Find a cool, shaded spot or a warm indoor location to take a break.

- **Seek Shelter in Severe Weather:** If a thunderstorm or other severe weather hits, seek shelter immediately. Avoid tall objects, open fields, and bodies of water during thunderstorms.

If you're caught in a storm, find shelter in a sturdy building or vehicle.

- **Know When to Stop**: If the weather becomes too dangerous, stop canvassing and seek shelter. It's better to reschedule your canvassing efforts than to put yourself at risk.

## What to Do If You Encounter Hostile Individuals or Unsafe Environments

While most people you encounter while canvassing will be polite or indifferent, there may be times when you encounter hostile individuals or find yourself in an unsafe environment. Knowing how to handle these situations calmly and effectively is essential for your safety.

### 1. Recognizing Potentially Hostile Situations

Hostility can manifest in various ways, from verbal aggression to physical intimidation. It's important to recognize the signs of a potentially hostile situation so you can take appropriate action.

Signs of Hostility:

- **Aggressive Language or Tone:** If someone speaks to you in a raised voice, uses threatening language, or makes derogatory remarks, they may be hostile.

- **Physical Intimidation:** Body language such as standing too close, blocking your path, or making threatening gestures can indicate hostility.

- **Verbal Threats:** Direct threats of violence or harm should be taken seriously and reported to authorities immediately.

- **Group Behavior:** Groups of people, especially if they appear agitated or confrontational, can pose a higher risk of hostility.

## 2. Steps to Take When Confronted by a Hostile Individual

If you encounter a hostile individual, your primary goal is to de-escalate the situation and remove yourself from danger.

De-Escalation Techniques:

- **Stay Calm and Non-Confrontational:** Maintain a calm demeanor and avoid raising your voice or engaging in a confrontational manner. Speak slowly and softly to help defuse the situation.

- **Acknowledge Their Feelings:** Show that you understand their frustration or anger without agreeing with their viewpoint. For example, "I can see that you're upset, and I'm sorry that you feel this way."

- **Avoid Arguing:** Resist the urge to argue or defend your position. Instead, focus on finding a way to end the conversation peacefully. For example, "I understand that we have different opinions. I'll leave you to your day."

- **Create Distance:** If you feel physically threatened, create distance between yourself and the individual. Step back slowly and calmly, and look for an exit route.

- **Leave the Area:** If the situation doesn't improve or if the person becomes more aggressive, leave the area immediately. Walk away calmly, and do not engage further.

## 3. Encountering Unsafe Environments

In addition to hostile individuals, you may encounter environments that feel unsafe due to factors such as high crime rates, poor lighting, or isolated locations. It's important to trust your instincts and take action to protect yourself.

Steps to Take in Unsafe Environments:

- **Assess the Area:** Before canvassing in a new area, assess the environment for potential risks. Look for signs such as broken windows, graffiti, or groups of loitering individuals that may indicate a higher risk of crime.

- **Stick to Well-Traveled Areas:** Avoid isolated or poorly lit areas, especially after dark. Stick to well-traveled streets and neighborhoods where there are more people around.

- **Canvass with a Partner:** Canvassing with a partner or group provides an added layer of safety. If you're in an area that feels unsafe, having someone with you can help deter potential threats.

- **Know Your Exits:** Be aware of your surroundings and identify exit routes in case you need to leave quickly. Stay close to main roads and avoid dead-end streets or alleys.

- **Leave If You Feel Unsafe:** If you feel uncomfortable or unsafe in an area, trust your instincts and leave immediately. It's better to err on the side of caution and reschedule your canvassing for another time.

## Dealing with Legal Issues or Law Enforcement Encounters

While canvassing is a legal and protected activity, there may be times when you encounter legal issues or interact with law enforcement. Understanding your rights and knowing how to handle these situations can help you navigate them smoothly.

## 1. Understanding Your Legal Rights as a Canvasser

As a canvasser, you have certain legal rights that protect your ability to engage with voters and promote your candidate or cause. However, it's important to be aware of any local laws or regulations that may affect your activities.

Key Legal Rights:

- **Freedom of Speech:** The First Amendment of the U.S. Constitution protects your right to free speech, including political canvassing. This means you have the right to knock on doors, distribute literature, and engage with voters.

- **Access to Public Spaces:** Canvassers generally have the right to access public spaces, such as sidewalks and parks, for their activities. However, private property, such as apartment complexes or gated communities, may have restrictions.

- **No Solicitation Laws:** Some areas have "no solicitation" laws or signs, which may restrict certain types of canvassing. It's important to know the local regulations and respect any posted signs.

- **Permits:** In some cities or towns, canvassers may be required to obtain a permit before engaging in door-to-door activities. Check with your campaign headquarters to ensure you have the necessary permits if required.

## 2. Interacting with Law Enforcement

While most interactions with law enforcement will be routine, it's important to know how to handle the situation if you're approached by a police officer or other authority figure while canvassing.

Steps to Take When Interacting with Law Enforcement:

- **Stay Calm and Respectful:** If approached by law enforcement, remain calm and respectful. Avoid sudden movements, and keep your hands visible at all times.

- **Identify Yourself:** Politely identify yourself as a canvasser working for [Candidate's Name]'s campaign. You may be asked to show identification or campaign materials to verify your role.

- **Know Your Rights:** If you're asked to stop canvassing or leave an area, politely ask if there is a specific law or ordinance that prohibits your activities. You have the right to ask for clarification and to continue canvassing if you are not in violation of any laws.

- **Comply with Lawful Orders:** If the officer gives you a lawful order, such as asking you to leave private property, comply with the request. You can always return to canvass in the area later, after verifying the legal requirements.

- **Document the Interaction:** If you believe your rights have been violated, document the interaction by noting the officer's name, badge number, and the details of the encounter. Report the incident to your campaign headquarters for further action.

## 3. Dealing with Legal Issues

If you encounter legal issues while canvassing, such as being accused of trespassing or violating local ordinances, it's important to handle the situation carefully.

Steps to Take When Facing Legal Issues:

- **Seek Legal Advice:** If you're facing legal issues, such as being charged with a violation, seek legal advice from the campaign's legal team or a qualified attorney. They can provide guidance on how to proceed and help protect your rights.

- **Document Everything:** Keep detailed records of the incident, including any interactions with law enforcement, witnesses, and any documentation you receive. This information will be important if you need to defend yourself legally.

- **Cooperate with Authorities:** Cooperate with authorities while protecting your rights. Provide necessary information, but avoid making statements that could be used against you later. It's often best to consult with legal counsel before making any formal statements.

- **Report to Headquarters:** Immediately report any legal issues to your campaign headquarters. They can provide support, including legal assistance, and help you navigate the situation.

**Staying Calm Under Pressure and Adapting on the Fly**

Unexpected situations often require you to think quickly and adapt to changing circumstances. Staying calm under pressure is essential for making sound decisions and ensuring your safety.

## 1. The Importance of Staying Calm

Staying calm in the face of unexpected challenges allows you to think clearly, assess the situation, and take appropriate action. Panic or stress can cloud your judgment and lead to poor decision-making.

Benefits of Staying Calm:

- **Improved Decision-Making:** A calm mind is better equipped to process information and make rational decisions. This is especially important in emergencies or high-pressure situations.

- **De-Escalation:** Remaining calm can help de-escalate tense situations, whether you're dealing with a hostile individual or navigating a challenging environment.

- **Increased Confidence:** Staying calm can boost your confidence and help you project a sense of control and competence, which can positively influence those around you.

## 2. Techniques for Staying Calm Under Pressure

There are several techniques you can use to stay calm when faced with unexpected challenges. Practicing these techniques regularly can help you remain composed when it matters most.

Calming Techniques:

- **Deep Breathing:** Deep breathing is one of the most effective ways to calm your nervous system. Take slow, deep breaths, inhaling through your nose and exhaling through your mouth. Focus on the rhythm of your breath to help clear your mind.

- **Mindfulness:** Mindfulness involves staying present in the moment and observing your thoughts and feelings without judgment. If you start to feel overwhelmed, take a moment to ground yourself by focusing on your surroundings and taking a few deep breaths.

- **Positive Self-Talk:** Replace negative or anxious thoughts with positive self-talk. Remind yourself that you're capable of handling the situation and that you've been trained to respond effectively. For example, "I can handle this. I know what to do."

- **Visualization:** Visualize yourself successfully navigating the situation. Imagine yourself staying calm, making the right decisions, and resolving the issue. Visualization can help reinforce your confidence and reduce stress.

- **Progressive Muscle Relaxation:** Progressive muscle relaxation involves tensing and then relaxing different muscle groups in your body. This technique can help release physical tension and promote a sense of calm.

## 3. Adapting to Changing Circumstances

Adaptability is the ability to adjust your approach when faced with new or unexpected challenges. Being adaptable allows you to respond effectively to changing circumstances and find creative solutions to problems.

Strategies for Adapting on the Fly:

- **Stay Flexible:** Be open to changing your plans or approach if the situation calls for it. Flexibility is key to adapting to new information or challenges. For example, if your planned route is blocked, be ready to adjust your canvassing route and find an alternative.

- **Prioritize Safety:** When adapting to a new situation, always prioritize safety. If conditions become too risky, it's okay to stop canvassing and regroup. Safety should always come first.

- **Think Creatively**: Sometimes, unexpected situations require creative solutions. Think outside the box and consider alternative ways to achieve your goals. For example, if weather conditions prevent door-to-door canvassing, consider switching to phone banking or organizing a virtual event.

- **Communicate with Your Team:** Keep your team informed of any changes or challenges you encounter. Clear communication ensures that everyone is on the same page and can adapt together. For example, if you decide to change your canvassing strategy due to an unexpected event, let your team know and discuss how to proceed.

- **Reflect and Learn:** After navigating an unexpected situation, take time to reflect on what happened and what you learned from the experience. Consider what worked well, what could have been done differently, and how you can apply those lessons in the future.

**Navigating the Unexpected with Confidence**

Dealing with unexpected situations is an inevitable part of canvassing, but with the right preparation and mindset, you can navigate these challenges with confidence. By understanding how to handle emergencies, respond to hostile individuals, manage legal issues, and stay calm under pressure, you'll be better equipped to adapt to any situation that comes your way.

Remember that every unexpected situation is an opportunity to learn and grow. The more experience you gain in handling these challenges, the more resilient and adaptable you'll become as a canvasser and as a member of your campaign team.

As you continue your canvassing efforts, keep these strategies in mind and trust in your ability to navigate the unexpected. By staying calm, thinking clearly, and prioritizing safety, you can overcome obstacles and continue making a positive impact on your community and your campaign.

# Chapter 11: Leveraging Technology

In today's digital age, technology has become an indispensable tool in political campaigns, enhancing traditional methods like doorknocking with cutting-edge solutions that make canvassing more efficient, data-driven, and impactful. Leveraging technology allows campaigners to optimize their efforts, track voter interactions, engage with voters through multiple channels, and stay updated on the latest developments in real-time.

## Using Mobile Apps and Digital Tools to Enhance Your Efforts

The advent of mobile apps and digital tools has revolutionized the way political campaigns are conducted, particularly in the area of canvassing. These tools streamline processes, provide real-time data, and help campaigners reach voters more effectively. Understanding how to use these tools can significantly enhance your doorknocking efforts.

### 1. The Benefits of Mobile Apps in Canvassing

Mobile apps designed specifically for canvassing provide a range of benefits that can help you maximize your effectiveness in the field. These apps are typically equipped with features that allow you to plan your routes, track voter interactions, and access important data on the go.

Key Benefits of Canvassing Apps:

- **Route Optimization:** Canvassing apps often include route optimization features, helping you plan the most efficient path through your assigned area. This saves time, reduces the physical strain of canvassing, and ensures that you can reach more voters in less time.

- **Real-Time Data Access:** With a canvassing app, you have access to real-time data, including voter demographics, past interactions, and important issues. This allows you to tailor your approach to each voter and stay informed about the most relevant talking points.

- **Voter Interaction Tracking:** Canvassing apps allow you to log voter interactions immediately after they happen, ensuring that no details are forgotten. You can record the voter's level of support, concerns, and any follow-up actions needed, all in one place.

- **Instant Updates**: Campaign headquarters can send instant updates and alerts through the app, ensuring that you're always in the loop about any changes in strategy or important developments.

- **Paperless Operation:** By using a digital tool, you can reduce the need for paper lists, maps, and notes, making your canvassing more environmentally friendly and reducing the risk of losing important information.

## 2. Popular Canvassing Apps and How to Use Them

There are several popular canvassing apps used by political campaigns, each offering a range of features to help you in the field. Understanding how to use these apps effectively can significantly boost your canvassing efforts.

**NationBuilder:** NationBuilder is a comprehensive platform that combines voter data management, canvassing, and digital engagement. The app allows you to track voter interactions, update contact details, and record notes on conversations. It also integrates with social media, helping you engage with voters online and offline.

- How to Use NationBuilder: Before heading out to canvass, use the app to review your assigned territory and familiarize yourself with voter profiles. As you canvass, log each interaction in the app, noting the voter's concerns and any follow-up needed. The app will sync this data with the campaign's central database in real-time.

**MiniVAN:** MiniVAN is one of the most widely used canvassing apps, particularly for large-scale campaigns. It allows you to access voter lists, log interactions, and update voter data in real-time. The app's offline mode ensures that you can continue canvassing even in areas with poor cell reception, with data syncing once you regain connectivity.

- How to Use MiniVAN: Download your list of assigned voters before heading out, ensuring you have access to the information even if you lose connectivity. As you knock on doors, use the app to mark whether the voter was home, how they responded, and any notes on the conversation. MiniVAN also allows you to track your progress and see which voters you've already visited.

**Outvote:** Outvote is an app that allows canvassers to combine traditional canvassing with peer-to-peer outreach. It enables you to identify friends and acquaintances who are voters in your district and engage with them directly. The app integrates social media, text messaging, and email to broaden your reach.

- How to Use Outvote: Sync your contacts with the app to identify potential voters within your network. Use the app's messaging tools to reach out to these voters, share campaign information, and encourage them to support your candidate. You can also use the app to log canvassing interactions and share updates with your campaign team.

**Ecanvasser:** Ecanvasser is another powerful canvassing tool that provides detailed voter profiles, route mapping, and team coordination features. The app also includes analytics tools, allowing you to measure the effectiveness of your canvassing efforts.

- **How to Use Ecanvasser:** Use the app to plan your canvassing route and familiarize yourself with voter profiles in your assigned area. As you engage with voters, use the app to log interactions, update voter information, and record any follow-up actions needed. After canvassing, review the analytics to assess your performance and identify areas for improvement.

## 3. Digital Tools for Volunteer Coordination and Communication

Beyond canvassing apps, there are a range of digital tools that can help you coordinate with other volunteers, communicate effectively, and ensure that your efforts are aligned with the broader campaign strategy.

**Slack:** Slack is a popular communication platform used by many campaigns to coordinate activities, share updates, and collaborate in real-time. It allows you to create channels for specific teams or topics, ensuring that information is shared efficiently and that everyone stays connected.

- How to Use Slack: Join the campaign's Slack workspace and familiarize yourself with the channels relevant to your role. Use Slack to communicate with your team, share your progress, and ask questions. The app's notification settings allow you to stay informed without being overwhelmed by messages.

**Google Workspace:** Google Workspace (formerly G Suite) offers a suite of tools, including Google Docs, Sheets, and Drive, that can be used to manage documents, track data, and collaborate with other team members. Google Calendar is particularly useful for scheduling canvassing shifts and coordinating with other volunteers.

- How to Use Google Workspace: Use Google Docs and Sheets to create and share canvassing materials, track voter data, and collaborate on reports. Google Drive provides a central location for storing and accessing important documents, ensuring that everyone has the information they need. Google Calendar can be used to schedule shifts, set reminders, and coordinate with other volunteers.

**Trello:** Trello is a project management tool that uses boards, lists, and cards to organize tasks and track progress. It's a versatile tool that can be used to manage everything from canvassing schedules to follow-up actions and event planning.

- How to Use Trello: Set up a Trello board for your canvassing team, with lists for tasks, in-progress actions, and completed items. Use cards to assign specific tasks to team members, track their progress, and ensure that nothing falls through the cracks. Trello's drag-and-drop interface makes it easy to update the board as tasks are completed.

**Zoom:** Zoom is a video conferencing tool that can be used for virtual team meetings, training sessions, and strategy discussions. It's an essential tool for staying connected with your team, especially if you're working remotely or coordinating with volunteers in different locations.

- How to Use Zoom: Schedule regular Zoom meetings to check in with your team, discuss progress, and plan upcoming canvassing activities. Use Zoom's screen-sharing feature to present data, share resources, and collaborate on strategy. Recording meetings can also be helpful for those who can't attend live.

**How to Track Voter Interactions and Follow-Up Actions**

Tracking voter interactions and following up with potential supporters is a critical component of successful canvassing. By keeping detailed records of your conversations and ensuring that follow-up actions are completed, you can build stronger relationships with voters and increase the likelihood of securing their support.

## 1. The Importance of Detailed Voter Tracking

Tracking voter interactions allows you to build a comprehensive picture of each voter's preferences, concerns, and level of support. This information is invaluable for tailoring future outreach efforts and ensuring that no voter slips through the cracks.

Why Voter Tracking Matters:

- **Personalized Follow-Up:** Detailed records allow you to follow up with voters in a personalized way, addressing their specific concerns and building on your previous conversations.

- **Data-Driven Decision Making:** Voter tracking data provides insights into voter trends, helping the campaign refine its strategy and allocate resources more effectively.

- **Accountability:** Keeping detailed records ensures that follow-up actions are completed and that all team members are accountable for their assigned tasks.

- **Maximizing Impact:** By tracking interactions, you can focus your efforts on undecided voters, those who need more information, or those who have expressed interest in volunteering or attending events.

## 2. Best Practices for Recording Voter Interactions

To get the most out of your voter tracking efforts, it's important to follow best practices for recording interactions and maintaining accurate, up-to-date records.

What to Record During Voter Interactions:

- **Voter Contact Information:** Ensure that you have accurate contact information for each voter, including their name, address, phone number, and email address. This is essential for follow-up actions and future outreach.

- **Level of Support:** Record the voter's level of support for your candidate or cause. Many canvassing apps use a scale (e.g., strong supporter, lean supporter, undecided, lean opponent, strong opponent) to categorize voters. This information helps prioritize follow-up efforts.

- **Key Issues and Concerns:** Note any specific issues or concerns the voter mentioned during the conversation. This allows you to address these issues in future communications and provides valuable data for the campaign's policy team.

- **Action Items:** If the voter requested additional information, expressed interest in volunteering, or mentioned any other follow-up action, make sure to record these items clearly. Assign deadlines and responsible team members for each action item.

- **Interaction Details:** Record any other relevant details from the interaction, such as the voter's demeanor, any personal stories they shared, or the overall tone of the conversation. These notes can help you build rapport in future interactions.

### 3. Automating Follow-Up Actions

With the help of digital tools, you can automate many of the follow-up actions required after voter interactions.

Automation helps ensure that no tasks are forgotten and allows you to manage your time more effectively.

Automating Follow-Up Actions:

- **Email Automation:** Use email automation tools, such as Mailchimp or Constant Contact, to send follow-up emails to voters. You can create templates for different scenarios (e.g., providing more information, thanking a new supporter, confirming a volunteer sign-up) and schedule emails to be sent automatically based on the voter's response.

- **Text Message Automation:** Platforms like Hustle or Textedly allow you to send personalized text messages to voters as a follow-up to your canvassing interactions. These tools enable you to reach voters quickly and efficiently, with the option to automate responses based on their replies.

- **Task Management:** Use a task management tool like Trello or Asana to assign follow-up actions to team members. Set due dates and reminders to ensure that tasks are completed on time. For example, if a voter requested more information on a specific policy, you can assign the task of sending that information to the appropriate team member.

## 4. Reviewing and Analyzing Voter Data

Regularly reviewing and analyzing your voter tracking data is essential for identifying trends, refining your approach, and making data-driven decisions that enhance your canvassing efforts.

How to Review and Analyze Voter Data:

- **Voter Segmentation:** Segment voters based on their level of support, key issues, and demographic information. This allows you to tailor your messaging and prioritize outreach to undecided or swing voters.

- **Trend Analysis:** Look for trends in the data, such as common concerns among voters in a particular area or demographic. This information can help the campaign adjust its messaging and focus on the issues that matter most to voters.

- **Performance Metrics:** Track key performance metrics, such as the number of voters contacted, the percentage of undecided voters who were persuaded, and the success rate of follow-up actions. Use this data to evaluate the effectiveness of your canvassing efforts and identify areas for improvement.

- **Reporting:** Regularly share your findings with campaign headquarters and other team members. Clear and concise reports ensure that everyone is informed about the progress of the canvassing efforts and can contribute to refining the strategy.

## The Role of Social Media in Supplementing Your Doorknocking Efforts

While doorknocking is an essential component of voter outreach, social media provides an additional platform to engage with voters, share campaign messages, and build community support. By integrating social media into your canvassing efforts, you can reach a broader audience and reinforce your message across multiple channels.

## 1. Social Media as a Campaign Tool

Social media platforms like Facebook, Twitter, Instagram, and TikTok have become powerful tools for political campaigns, allowing candidates and volunteers to connect with voters, share content, and mobilize supporters.

Benefits of Using Social Media in Campaigning:

- **Broad Reach:** Social media allows you to reach a wide audience, including people who may not be home when you knock on their door or who live outside your immediate canvassing area.

- **Real-Time Engagement:** Social media enables real-time engagement with voters, allowing you to respond to questions, share updates, and participate in conversations as they happen.

- **Amplification of Your Message:** Content shared on social media can be liked, shared, and commented on, amplifying your message beyond your immediate network and reaching new potential supporters.

- **Community Building:** Social media provides a platform for building a sense of community among supporters, where they can share their experiences, discuss issues, and organize events.

- **Visual Storytelling:** Platforms like Instagram and TikTok allow you to tell your campaign's story through visuals, whether it's photos of canvassing efforts, videos of the candidate speaking on key issues, or graphics highlighting policy positions.

## 2. Integrating Social Media with Doorknocking

By integrating social media with your doorknocking efforts, you can create a cohesive outreach strategy that engages voters both online and offline.

Strategies for Integrating Social Media:

- **Promote Events:** Use social media to promote canvassing events, rallies, and other campaign activities. Share details about when and where you'll be canvassing, and encourage supporters to join you or follow your progress online.

- **Share Your Experience:** Document your canvassing efforts by posting photos, videos, or stories on social media. Share highlights from your conversations with voters, insights into what issues are resonating with the community, and personal reflections on the experience.

- **Engage with Voters Online:** After doorknocking, follow up with voters on social media. Send them a thank-you message, answer any questions they might have, and encourage them to stay connected with the campaign through your social media channels.

- **Leverage Hashtags:** Use campaign-specific hashtags to connect your social media content with broader campaign efforts. This makes it easier for supporters to find and engage with your content and helps create a sense of unity across the campaign.

- **Encourage Sharing:** Encourage voters and supporters to share their own experiences on social media using the campaign's hashtags. User-generated content can help spread your message and show the breadth of support for your candidate.

## 3. Engaging with Voters Through Social Media

Engaging with voters through social media is about more than just broadcasting messages—it's about building relationships, listening to concerns, and fostering a sense of community.

Tips for Effective Social Media Engagement:

- **Be Responsive:** Respond to comments, messages, and questions from voters in a timely manner. Even a simple acknowledgment can go a long way in building rapport and showing that you value their input.

- **Listen and Learn:** Use social media as a listening tool to understand what voters are saying about the campaign, the issues that matter to them, and their perceptions of the candidate. This information can inform your canvassing efforts and help you address voters' concerns more effectively.

- **Share Valuable Content:** Share content that is informative, engaging, and relevant to your audience. This might include policy explanations, event updates, voter registration information, or behind-the-scenes glimpses of the campaign.

- **Encourage Dialogue:** Create opportunities for voters to engage in dialogue, whether it's through polls, Q&A sessions, or live chats with the candidate. Encouraging voter participation fosters a sense of ownership and involvement in the campaign.

- **Be Authentic:** Authenticity is key on social media. Be genuine in your interactions, share personal stories, and let your passion for the campaign shine through. Voters are more likely to connect with a campaign that feels relatable and sincere.

## 4. Measuring Social Media Impact

Just as with doorknocking, it's important to measure the impact of your social media efforts to ensure that they are contributing effectively to the campaign's goals.

How to Measure Social Media Impact:

- **Engagement Metrics:** Track metrics such as likes, shares, comments, and followers to gauge how well your content is resonating with your audience. High engagement indicates that voters are interested and invested in your message.

- Reach and Impressions: Measure the reach and impressions of your social media posts to understand how many people are seeing your content. This helps you assess the effectiveness of your social media strategy in reaching new voters.

- **Click-Through Rates:** If you're sharing links to campaign resources, events, or donation pages, track the click-through rates to see how many people are taking action based on your social media content.

- **Sentiment Analysis:** Use sentiment analysis tools to monitor the tone of conversations about your campaign on social media. Positive sentiment indicates that your message is being well-received, while negative sentiment can highlight areas for improvement.

- **Conversion Tracking:** If your goal is to drive specific actions, such as signing up for a volunteer shift or making a donation, track conversions to see how well your social media efforts are driving these outcomes.

## Staying Updated on Real-Time Campaign Data and Strategy Shifts

In a fast-paced campaign environment, staying updated on real-time data and strategy shifts is essential for ensuring that your efforts are aligned with the broader campaign goals. Access to real-time information allows you to adapt quickly, make informed decisions, and maximize your impact.

### 1. The Importance of Real-Time Data

Real-time data provides a snapshot of the campaign's current status, including voter outreach progress, support levels, and key issues. This data is crucial for making informed decisions and adjusting your strategy as needed.

Why Real-Time Data Matters:

- **Informed Decision-Making:** Access to real-time data allows you to make informed decisions about where to focus your efforts, which voters to prioritize, and how to allocate resources.

- **Quick Adaptation:** In a rapidly changing campaign environment, being able to adapt quickly to new information is crucial. Real-time data allows you to respond to emerging trends, voter concerns, or shifts in public opinion.

- **Maximizing Efficiency:** By staying updated on the latest data, you can ensure that your efforts are targeted and efficient, avoiding wasted time and resources.

## 2. Tools for Accessing Real-Time Campaign Data

Several tools and platforms provide access to real-time campaign data, helping you stay informed and adjust your strategy on the fly.

**Campaign Dashboard:** Many campaigns use a centralized dashboard that provides real-time data on voter outreach, volunteer activities, fundraising, and other key metrics. This dashboard is typically accessible through a web portal or mobile app.

- How to Use the Campaign Dashboard: Log in to the campaign's dashboard regularly to monitor your progress and stay updated on the latest data. Use the dashboard to track key performance indicators (KPIs), such as the number of voters contacted, the level of support, and the success rate of follow-up actions.

**Data Analytics Platforms:** Platforms like NationBuilder, VAN, or Ecanvasser offer robust data analytics tools that allow you to analyze voter data, track trends, and measure the impact of your efforts.

- How to Use Data Analytics Platforms: Use the platform's analytics tools to segment voters, analyze trends, and identify opportunities for improvement. These platforms often provide visualizations, such as charts and graphs, that make it easy to interpret the data and share insights with your team.

**Communication Tools:** Tools like Slack, Zoom, or WhatsApp can be used to receive real-time updates from campaign headquarters, share data with your team, and coordinate strategy shifts.

- How to Use Communication Tools for Real-Time Updates: Set up notifications in your communication tools to receive instant updates from headquarters. Use these tools to discuss strategy shifts with your team and ensure that everyone is aligned with the latest information.

## 3. Responding to Strategy Shifts

Campaign strategies can shift quickly in response to new data, voter feedback, or external events. Being able to respond to these shifts effectively is essential for staying on track and maximizing your impact.

How to Respond to Strategy Shifts:

- **Stay Flexible:** Be prepared to adjust your approach as the campaign strategy evolves. This might involve changing your messaging, focusing on different voter demographics, or reallocating resources to new areas.

- **Communicate Clearly:** When a strategy shift occurs, communicate clearly with your team to ensure that everyone understands the new direction and their role in implementing it. Use communication tools to share updates and provide guidance on how to proceed.

- **Review and Reflect:** After implementing a strategy shift, review the results and reflect on what worked and what didn't. Use this feedback to refine your approach and improve future efforts.

- **Stay Aligned with Campaign Goals:** Keep the campaign's overall goals in mind as you adapt to strategy shifts. Ensure that your efforts are always aligned with the broader objectives and that you're contributing to the campaign's success.

## Maximizing Impact Through Technology

Leveraging technology in your canvassing efforts is no longer an option—it's a necessity in the modern political landscape. By using mobile apps, digital tools, and social media, you can enhance your doorknocking efforts, track voter interactions, engage with a broader audience, and stay updated on real-time data and strategy shifts.

The integration of technology allows you to work more efficiently, make data-driven decisions, and adapt quickly to changing circumstances. As you continue your canvassing efforts, embrace the tools and platforms available to you, and use them to maximize your impact on the campaign.

Remember that technology is a powerful tool, but it's the human connection that ultimately drives voter engagement and support. Use technology to enhance your interactions, build relationships, and create a meaningful impact in your community. By combining the best of both worlds—traditional canvassing methods and modern digital tools—you can contribute to a successful and effective campaign.

# Chapter 12: Post-Visit Follow-Up

The job of a canvasser doesn't end when you walk away from a voter's door. In many ways, that first conversation is just the beginning. Post-visit follow-up is crucial to converting undecided voters, solidifying support, and ensuring that the efforts of the campaign have a lasting impact.

## The Importance of Timely Follow-Up with Undecided Voters

Voter outreach is about building relationships, and like any relationship, it requires ongoing communication and attention. Timely follow-up is essential for maintaining the momentum of your initial contact and for making the most of the opportunities that each interaction presents.

### 1. Reinforcing the Message

When you engage with a voter, especially an undecided one, the conversation often ends with more questions or the need for additional information. A timely follow-up allows you to reinforce your message while the conversation is still fresh in the voter's mind.

Why Timely Follow-Up Matters:

- **Strengthening Connections:** Following up promptly shows that you care about the voter's concerns and are committed to providing them with the information they need. This can help build trust and move the voter closer to supporting your candidate.

- **Addressing Concerns:** Many undecided voters have specific concerns or questions that may not be fully addressed during the initial conversation. A timely follow-up gives you the chance to provide the necessary information and alleviate any doubts.

- **Capitalizing on Interest:** If a voter expresses interest in your candidate or an issue during your conversation, it's important to act quickly. Timely follow-up ensures that you capitalize on that interest before it wanes or is overshadowed by other events or conversations.

## 2. Converting Undecided Voters

Undecided voters are often the key to winning elections, especially in closely contested races. Following up with these voters can be the difference between securing their support and losing their vote to an opponent.

Strategies for Converting Undecided Voters:

- **Personalized Follow-Up:** Tailor your follow-up to the specific concerns and interests expressed by the voter. This could involve sending them additional information on a particular issue, inviting them to a campaign event, or offering to connect them with someone who can address their questions in more detail.

- **Multiple Touchpoints:** Sometimes, one follow-up isn't enough. Consider multiple touchpoints, such as a follow-up email, a phone call, and another visit closer to Election Day.

This sustained engagement can help keep your candidate top of mind.

- **Provide Clear Calls to Action:** Make it easy for undecided voters to take the next step by providing clear calls to action in your follow-up communications. This could be as simple as encouraging them to visit your candidate's website for more information, attend a local event, or sign up for a mailing list.

- **Acknowledge and Respect Their Process:** Understand that making a decision can take time, and some voters may need more information or further engagement before they feel ready to commit. Respect their process and be patient, but remain proactive in offering support and information.

## Methods for Tracking and Organizing Follow-Up Tasks

Effective follow-up requires organization and consistency. Without a reliable system for tracking your tasks and progress, it's easy for important follow-up actions to slip through the cracks. This section will explore methods and tools for keeping your follow-up efforts organized and on track.

### 1. Using Digital Tools for Task Management

Digital tools can streamline your follow-up efforts by providing a centralized platform for tracking tasks, setting reminders, and ensuring accountability. These tools range from simple to-do lists to more sophisticated project management software.

Popular Digital Tools for Task Management:

- **Trello:** Trello is a flexible project management tool that uses boards, lists, and cards to help you organize your tasks. You can create a board specifically for follow-up tasks, with lists for different stages of the process (e.g., tasks to be done, in progress, completed).

- **Asana:** Asana is another powerful tool that allows you to create tasks, set deadlines, assign responsibilities, and track progress. It's particularly useful if you're coordinating follow-up efforts with a team, as it provides clear visibility into who is responsible for each task.

- **Google Tasks:** For a simpler approach, Google Tasks integrates with Gmail and Google Calendar, allowing you to create to-do lists, set due dates, and link tasks to specific emails or calendar events. This can be particularly useful for managing follow-up communications.

- **CRM Systems:** Many campaigns use Customer Relationship Management (CRM) systems like NationBuilder or NGP VAN, which include built-in tools for tracking voter interactions and follow-up tasks. These systems allow you to log each interaction, set follow-up reminders, and track the progress of each voter through the engagement process.

## 2. Setting Priorities and Deadlines

Not all follow-up tasks are created equal. Some may require immediate attention, while others can be scheduled for later. Setting priorities and deadlines ensures that the most important tasks are completed on time and that you stay on top of your follow-up efforts.

Strategies for Prioritizing Follow-Up Tasks:

- **Urgency and Importance:** Use the Eisenhower Matrix to prioritize tasks based on urgency and importance. Tasks that are both urgent and important should be your top priority, while tasks that are less urgent can be scheduled for later.

- **Voter Support Level:** Prioritize follow-up with undecided voters or those who have expressed interest but haven't yet committed. These voters are more likely to be swayed by timely and personalized follow-up.

- **Key Issues:** If a voter has expressed concern about a key issue that could impact their support for your candidate, make follow-up on that issue a priority. Addressing their concerns promptly can be crucial in securing their vote.

- **Event Timing:** If your follow-up involves inviting voters to an upcoming event, prioritize those tasks based on the event date to ensure they receive the information in time.

## 3. Automating Follow-Up Communications

Automation can help ensure that your follow-up tasks are completed on time, even if you're juggling multiple responsibilities. By setting up automated emails, text messages, or reminders, you can maintain consistent communication with voters without overwhelming yourself.

How to Automate Follow-Up Communications:

- **Email Automation:** Use email marketing tools like Mailchimp or Constant Contact to set up automated email sequences. For example, you can create a series of follow-up emails that are triggered by specific voter interactions, such as signing up for more information or attending an event.

- **Text Message Automation:** Platforms like Hustle or Textedly allow you to send personalized text messages to voters as part of your follow-up strategy. These tools often include features for automating responses based on keywords or voter actions.

- **Reminder Systems:** Use calendar tools or task management apps to set reminders for manual follow-up tasks, such as making a phone call or sending a personalized email. Automating reminders helps ensure that nothing slips through the cracks.

**How to Use Voter Feedback to Improve Future Interactions**

Voter feedback is an invaluable resource for refining your approach and improving future interactions. By analyzing the feedback you receive and using it to inform your strategy, you can become a more effective canvasser and contribute more significantly to your campaign's success.

**1. Collecting and Recording Voter Feedback**

The first step in using voter feedback is to collect it systematically during your interactions and ensure it's recorded accurately. Feedback can come in many forms, from direct comments and concerns to more subtle cues like body language or tone of voice.

Ways to Collect Voter Feedback:

- **Direct Questions:** Don't be afraid to ask voters directly for their feedback. Questions like "What issues are most important to you?" or "How do you feel about our candidate's stance on [issue]?" can provide valuable insights into their priorities and concerns.

- **Observation:** Pay attention to non-verbal cues, such as a voter's body language, facial expressions, or tone of voice. These can often reveal how they're really feeling, even if they don't express it directly.

- **Follow-Up Surveys:** Consider sending a short survey as part of your follow-up communication. Surveys can be a quick and effective way to gather feedback on specific issues or the voter's overall experience with your campaign.

- **Logging Feedback:** Ensure that all feedback, whether direct or observed, is logged in your canvassing app or CRM system. This ensures that the information is available for future interactions and can be analyzed to inform broader campaign strategies.

## 2. Analyzing Voter Feedback

Once you've collected voter feedback, the next step is to analyze it for patterns, trends, and actionable insights. This analysis can help you identify what's working, what's not, and how you can improve your approach.

How to Analyze Voter Feedback:

- **Identify Common Concerns:** Look for recurring themes in the feedback you receive. Are multiple voters expressing concern about the same issue? Are there common questions that need to be addressed more clearly? Identifying these patterns can help you refine your messaging and address the most pressing concerns.

- **Segment Feedback by Demographics:** Analyze feedback by voter demographics, such as age, location, or political affiliation. This can help you understand how different groups of voters perceive your candidate and tailor your approach accordingly.

- **Compare Positive and Negative Feedback:** Compare positive and negative feedback to understand what's resonating with voters and what's causing hesitation. Use this analysis to amplify the messages that are working and address any weaknesses in your approach.

- **Assess the Impact of Follow-Up:** If you've already conducted follow-up with some voters, compare the feedback before and after to assess the impact of your efforts. This can help you refine your follow-up strategy and improve your effectiveness in future interactions.

### 3. Using Feedback to Improve Future Interactions

The ultimate goal of collecting and analyzing voter feedback is to use it to improve your future interactions. By incorporating what you've learned into your approach, you can become a more effective communicator and better advocate for your candidate.

Strategies for Using Feedback to Improve:

- **Refine Your Messaging:** Use feedback to refine your talking points and messaging. If voters consistently express confusion or concern about a particular issue, work on clarifying your explanation and addressing their concerns more effectively.

- **Tailor Your Approach:** Adjust your approach based on the specific needs and preferences of different voter segments. For example, if younger voters are particularly concerned about climate change, make sure to emphasize your candidate's environmental policies in your conversations with them.

- **Improve Your Listening Skills:** Feedback can also help you identify areas where you can improve your listening skills. If voters express frustration that their concerns aren't being heard, focus on active listening and ensuring that you're addressing their specific issues.

- **Enhance Your Follow-Up Strategy:** If voters appreciate timely follow-up but express a desire for more detailed information, consider providing more comprehensive resources in your follow-up communications. This could include links to policy papers, video explanations, or opportunities to engage with the campaign further.

## Communicating Your Results Back to the Campaign Team

Effective communication with your campaign team is essential for ensuring that your efforts are aligned with the broader campaign strategy and that valuable insights are shared across the organization. By regularly reporting your results and feedback, you can contribute to the campaign's overall success.

## 1. The Importance of Reporting Back

Reporting your results and insights back to the campaign team ensures that the valuable information you've gathered is used to inform campaign decisions, refine strategies, and allocate resources effectively.

Why Reporting Back Matters:

- **Data-Driven Decision Making:** Your on-the-ground insights provide the campaign with real-time data that can be used to make informed decisions about strategy, messaging, and resource allocation.

- **Feedback Loop:** Reporting back creates a feedback loop that helps the campaign continuously improve its approach. Your insights can inform adjustments to the campaign's messaging, targeting, and follow-up strategies.

- **Accountability and Transparency:** Regular reporting ensures accountability and transparency within the campaign. It allows team members to see the progress being made, understand the challenges faced, and work together to address them.

## 2. Methods for Communicating Results

There are several methods for communicating your results and feedback to the campaign team, ranging from formal reports to more informal updates. The key is to ensure that the information is communicated clearly and in a way that's actionable for the team.

Ways to Communicate Your Results:

- **Weekly or Daily Reports:** Create a regular report that summarizes your canvassing activities, voter feedback, and follow-up progress. This report can be shared with campaign leadership and relevant team members to keep everyone informed.

- **Team Meetings:** Participate in regular team meetings where you can share your insights and discuss your progress with other canvassers and campaign staff. This allows for real-time discussion and collaboration on any issues that arise.

- **CRM System Updates:** If your campaign uses a CRM system like NationBuilder or NGP VAN, ensure that all voter interactions, feedback, and follow-up tasks are logged in the system. This provides the campaign with a centralized source of data that can be analyzed and used to inform strategy.

- **Slack or Communication Channels:** Use tools like Slack to share quick updates, insights, or important information with your team. These platforms allow for ongoing communication and ensure that everyone stays connected and informed.

## 3. Providing Actionable Insights

When communicating your results, it's important to focus on providing actionable insights that can help the campaign improve its efforts and achieve its goals. This means going beyond just reporting data and offering specific recommendations based on your findings.

How to Provide Actionable Insights:

- **Highlight Key Takeaways:** In your reports or updates, highlight the key takeaways from your voter interactions and feedback. What are the most important trends or patterns? What issues are resonating most with voters? What challenges need to be addressed?

- **Offer Recommendations:** Based on your insights, offer specific recommendations for how the campaign can improve its strategy. For example, if you've noticed that voters are particularly concerned about healthcare, you might recommend increasing the emphasis on the candidate's healthcare policies in future messaging.

- **Support Recommendations with Data:** Wherever possible, support your recommendations with data. This could include statistics from your voter interactions, quotes from voters, or comparisons of different approaches. Data-driven insights are more persuasive and can help the campaign make informed decisions.

- **Be Solution-Oriented:** When identifying challenges or areas for improvement, focus on providing solutions rather than just pointing out problems. For example, if you've encountered resistance to a particular policy, suggest ways to reframe the issue or provide additional context to help voters understand its benefits.

## The Power of Effective Follow-Up

Post-visit follow-up is a critical component of any successful canvassing effort. By following up with undecided voters, tracking and organizing your tasks, using feedback to improve your approach, and communicating your results back to the campaign team, you can significantly increase the impact of your outreach and help drive the campaign toward victory.

Remember that follow-up is not just a task to check off your list—it's an opportunity to build deeper connections with voters, address their concerns, and move them closer to supporting your candidate. By approaching follow-up with the same dedication and attention to detail that you bring to your initial interactions, you can ensure that your efforts have a lasting and meaningful impact.

As you continue your canvassing efforts, keep these principles in mind and strive to make each follow-up interaction as effective and impactful as possible. By doing so, you'll be contributing not only to the success of your campaign but also to the broader goal of engaging and empowering voters in your community.

# Chapter 13: Maximizing Impact with Community Events

Doorknocking is an essential tool in grassroots campaigning, but to truly maximize your impact, it should be integrated with other outreach efforts, particularly community events and rallies. These gatherings provide a unique opportunity to engage with voters in a more dynamic, communal setting, allowing you to build relationships, share your candidate's message more effectively, and strengthen your campaign's presence within the community. This chapter will explore strategies for integrating doorknocking with local events, using community gatherings to engage with voters, coordinating with other campaign efforts like phone banking and mailers, and emphasizing the importance of maintaining visibility in the community.

## How to Integrate Doorknocking with Local Events and Rallies

Community events and rallies are often the heart of a political campaign's local outreach strategy. They bring people together, foster a sense of collective purpose, and create an environment where political messages can resonate more deeply. Integrating your doorknocking efforts with these events can amplify your impact by reinforcing your candidate's visibility and message across multiple channels.

### 1. Planning Around Local Events

The first step in integrating doorknocking with local events is to plan your canvassing efforts around these gatherings. This ensures that you can leverage the energy and focus of the event to enhance your outreach.

Strategies for Planning Around Local Events:

- **Identify Key Events:** Start by identifying key events in your community, such as town hall meetings, local fairs, cultural festivals, parades, or rallies. These events typically draw large crowds and provide a valuable opportunity to engage with a diverse cross-section of the community.

- **Coordinate with Event Organizers:** Reach out to event organizers to see how your campaign can participate. This might involve setting up a booth, distributing literature, or having your candidate speak at the event. Coordinating with organizers also ensures that your efforts align with the event's goals and flow smoothly.

- **Schedule Canvassing Before and After Events:** Schedule doorknocking efforts before and after major events to maximize your reach. Before the event, canvass in the surrounding neighborhoods to inform residents about the event and encourage them to attend. After the event, follow up with attendees or nearby residents to reinforce the messages shared at the event.

- **Use Events as Launch Points:** Consider using a community event as a launch point for a doorknocking campaign. Gather your volunteers at the event, energize them with a rally or speech, and then send them out to canvass the surrounding area. This approach can create a sense of momentum and purpose.

## 2. Integrating Messaging Across Channels

To make the most of the synergy between doorknocking and community events, it's important to integrate your messaging across all channels. This ensures consistency and reinforces your campaign's key themes and goals.

How to Integrate Messaging:

- **Develop a Unified Message:** Work with your campaign team to develop a unified message that can be communicated consistently across doorknocking, events, and other outreach efforts. This message should reflect your candidate's core values and key issues.

- **Coordinate Literature and Materials:** Ensure that the literature and materials used in doorknocking efforts are aligned with those distributed at events. This might include flyers, brochures, or handouts that highlight the same key points and calls to action.

- **Leverage Visual Branding:** Use consistent visual branding, such as logos, colors, and slogans, across all platforms. This helps create a cohesive identity for your campaign and makes it easier for voters to recognize and remember your candidate.

- **Reinforce Event Themes During Doorknocking:** If your campaign is focusing on a specific issue during an event, such as healthcare or education, make sure to reinforce that theme during your doorknocking efforts. This can help tie the event's message to individual voter interactions, making the message more impactful.

## 3. Engaging Volunteers and Supporters

Integrating doorknocking with community events is not only about outreach to voters—it's also a powerful way to engage and mobilize your volunteers and supporters.

Ways to Engage Volunteers:

- **Pre-Event Training and Briefings:** Before an event, hold training sessions or briefings for your volunteers. This prepares them to effectively engage with event attendees and provides them with the information and tools they need to canvas successfully afterward.

- **Create a Sense of Purpose:** Use the energy and excitement of community events to create a sense of purpose among your volunteers. Rally them with speeches, set clear goals for the day, and emphasize the impact their efforts will have on the campaign.

- **Provide Recognition and Rewards:** Recognize and reward volunteers who participate in both events and doorknocking efforts. This could be as simple as public acknowledgment at the event or offering small rewards like campaign merchandise or certificates of appreciation.

- **Encourage Social Sharing:** Encourage volunteers and supporters to share their experiences on social media. This helps spread the word about your campaign, showcases the enthusiasm of your base, and can attract new supporters.

## Using Community Gatherings as Opportunities to Engage with Voters

Community gatherings, whether large public events or smaller, more intimate meetings, offer unique opportunities to engage with voters in ways that aren't possible during traditional doorknocking. These events allow for deeper conversations, the chance to address broader audiences, and the opportunity to build a sense of community around your campaign.

### 1. The Power of Face-to-Face Engagement

Face-to-face engagement at community events allows you to connect with voters on a personal level, which can be incredibly persuasive. It's a chance to listen, respond to concerns, and build trust.

Benefits of Face-to-Face Engagement:

- **Building Trust:** Personal interactions help build trust between the voter and your campaign. When voters can see and hear your candidate or representatives in person, they are more likely to feel connected and take your message seriously.

- **Addressing Concerns Directly:** Events provide the opportunity to address voters' concerns directly. Whether through a Q&A session or informal conversations, you can clarify positions, dispel myths, and provide detailed answers that might not be possible in other settings.

- **Creating Memorable Experiences:** Engaging with voters in a community setting creates memorable experiences that can have a lasting impact. Whether it's a handshake from the candidate, a meaningful conversation, or even just being part of an enthusiastic crowd, these experiences can turn undecided voters into committed supporters.

## 2. Organizing and Participating in Community Events

Organizing or participating in community events requires careful planning and coordination. Whether you're hosting your own event or joining an existing one, it's important to ensure that your presence is impactful and aligns with your campaign goals.

Organizing Your Own Events:

- **Choose the Right Venue:** Select a venue that is accessible and comfortable for your target audience. Consider community centers, parks, or local businesses that are well-known in the area.

- **Plan Engaging Activities:** Plan activities that encourage voter participation and create opportunities for meaningful interactions. This might include town hall meetings, panel discussions, workshops, or informal meet-and-greets.

- **Promote the Event:** Use all available channels—social media, email, flyers, and word of mouth—to promote your event. Make sure that the event is well-publicized so that you attract a good turnout.

- **Prepare Your Team:** Ensure that your team is well-prepared to engage with attendees. This includes having talking points ready, being familiar with the event schedule, and knowing how to handle questions or concerns from the audience.

Participating in Existing Events:

- **Align with the Event's Purpose:** When participating in an existing event, ensure that your campaign's presence aligns with the event's purpose. For example, if you're attending a community health fair, focus on your candidate's healthcare policies and how they benefit the community.

- **Bring Value to the Event:** Contribute something of value to the event, whether it's an informative presentation, a booth with useful resources, or a team of volunteers to assist with event logistics. This helps create a positive association with your campaign.

- **Engage Actively:** Don't just be a passive participant. Actively engage with attendees, ask questions, and seek feedback. Use the opportunity to gather insights and build relationships with potential supporters.

- **Follow Up After the Event:** After the event, follow up with attendees who expressed interest in your campaign. This could be through email, social media, or even another face-to-face interaction.

## 3. Leveraging Small Community Gatherings

In addition to large events, small community gatherings such as neighborhood block parties, book clubs, or faith-based meetings offer valuable opportunities for more intimate and focused engagement.

Benefits of Small Gatherings:

- **Deeper Conversations:** Smaller gatherings allow for deeper, more personal conversations with voters. This can be particularly effective in addressing complex issues or converting undecided voters.

- **Targeted Outreach:** These events often attract specific demographics or interest groups, allowing you to tailor your message more precisely to the audience's concerns and priorities.

- **Building Stronger Relationships:** The intimacy of small gatherings fosters stronger, more personal relationships with voters. These relationships can lead to more sustained support and a network of advocates for your candidate within the community.

How to Engage in Small Gatherings:

- **Personal Invitations:** Encourage your volunteers and supporters to host small gatherings and invite friends, family, and neighbors. Personal invitations are often more effective than general advertising in getting people to attend.

- **Customize Your Approach:** Tailor your approach to the specific group or community you're engaging with. Research the group's interests and concerns beforehand so that you can address them directly in your conversations.

- **Encourage Dialogue:** Use small gatherings as an opportunity to foster dialogue rather than just deliver a message. Encourage attendees to share their views and ask questions, and make sure to listen as much as you speak.

## Coordinating with Other Campaign Efforts: Phone Banking, Mailers, and More

To maximize the impact of your outreach, it's essential to coordinate your doorknocking and event participation with other campaign efforts, such as phone banking, mailers, and digital outreach. This integrated approach ensures that your message reaches voters through multiple channels, reinforcing your campaign's visibility and effectiveness.

### 1. The Importance of Integrated Campaign Efforts

An integrated campaign strategy ensures that all outreach efforts work together to amplify your message and create a cohesive experience for voters. This approach helps to build recognition, reinforce key messages, and reach voters who may not be accessible through one method alone.

Benefits of an Integrated Campaign:

- **Reinforced Messaging:** When voters hear the same message through different channels—at their door, on the phone, in their mailbox, and online—it reinforces the campaign's key points and increases the likelihood that the message will stick.

- **Broader Reach:** Different voters respond to different forms of outreach. By coordinating doorknocking with other efforts, you can reach voters who may prefer one method over another, ensuring that your message is heard by a wider audience.

- **Consistency and Cohesion:** An integrated approach ensures consistency in your messaging and branding, creating a cohesive campaign that voters can easily recognize and connect with.

## 2. Coordinating Doorknocking with Phone Banking

Phone banking is a powerful tool that complements doorknocking by allowing you to reach voters who are not home when you visit or who live in areas that are difficult to canvass in person.

Strategies for Coordinating Doorknocking with Phone Banking:

- **Target Overlap:** Coordinate your doorknocking and phone banking efforts by targeting the same neighborhoods or voter segments. For example, if you knock on doors in a particular area, follow up with phone calls to those who weren't home or didn't answer.

- **Data Sharing:** Share data between your doorknocking and phone banking teams. Information gathered during phone calls can inform your doorknocking strategy and vice versa. This might include notes on voter concerns, support levels, or specific follow-up requests.

- **Pre-Event Phone Calls:** Use phone banking to invite voters to upcoming community events or rallies. This ensures a higher turnout and makes your doorknocking efforts more effective by building anticipation for the event.

- **Post-Event Follow-Up:** After an event, use phone banking to follow up with attendees or nearby residents. Reinforce the messages shared at the event and address any questions or concerns that arose.

## 3. Integrating Mailers with Doorknocking and Events

Mailers provide a tangible way to reach voters and can be a valuable complement to your doorknocking and event efforts. When coordinated effectively, mailers can reinforce the messages delivered in person and provide voters with information they can reference later.

How to Integrate Mailers with Other Efforts:

- **Pre-Event Mailers:** Send out mailers before a major event to inform voters of the event details and encourage attendance. This can be particularly effective in driving turnout and ensuring that your event has a strong impact.

- **Follow-Up Mailers:** After doorknocking or an event, send a follow-up mailer that reinforces the key messages and provides additional information. This could include a thank-you note, a summary of the candidate's positions, or a call to action such as volunteering or donating.

- **Targeted Mailers:** Use the data gathered from your doorknocking efforts to send targeted mailers to specific voter segments. For example, if you know that a certain neighborhood is particularly concerned about education, send them a mailer that focuses on your candidate's education policies.

- **Event Recap Mailers:** After a successful event, consider sending a mailer that recaps the event highlights and reinforces the campaign's key messages. This can help keep the momentum going and encourage further engagement from voters.

## 4. Leveraging Digital Outreach

Digital outreach, including social media, email campaigns, and online advertising, plays a crucial role in amplifying your message and reaching voters who are increasingly connected online.

Strategies for Coordinating Digital Outreach:

- **Event Promotion:** Use social media and email campaigns to promote upcoming events and rallies. Share event details, encourage RSVPs, and create online buzz to drive attendance.

- **Live Coverage and Updates:** Provide live coverage of events on social media, allowing supporters who can't attend in person to follow along and engage with the content. Post updates, photos, and videos to keep the online audience engaged.

- **Post-Event Content:** After an event, share content online that recaps the highlights, showcases the turnout, and reinforces the campaign's key messages. This content can be shared across multiple platforms, including social media, email, and the campaign website.

- **Digital Follow-Up:** Use email or social media to follow up with voters who attended an event or were engaged during doorknocking. Provide additional resources, answer questions, and encourage further involvement in the campaign.

## The Importance of Visibility and Presence in the Community

Maintaining a strong, consistent presence in the community is essential for building trust, credibility, and recognition for your campaign. Voters are more likely to support candidates who are visible, accessible, and actively engaged in the community.

### 1. Building a Strong Community Presence

A strong community presence goes beyond just showing up at events or knocking on doors. It's about becoming a trusted and recognized part of the community, someone voters can rely on to represent their interests and advocate for their needs.

Ways to Build a Strong Community Presence:

- **Regular Participation:** Make sure your campaign is regularly participating in community events, not just during election season but throughout the year. This demonstrates a genuine commitment to the community and helps build long-term relationships.

- **Volunteer Engagement:** Encourage your volunteers to be active in the community as well. When voters see campaign volunteers at local events, volunteering at community centers, or participating in local causes, it reinforces the campaign's commitment to the community.

- **Consistent Messaging:** Ensure that your messaging is consistent and aligned with the values and concerns of the community. This builds trust and ensures that voters know what your campaign stands for.

- **Community Partnerships:** Build partnerships with local organizations, businesses, and community leaders. These partnerships can help expand your reach, lend credibility to your campaign, and provide valuable insights into the community's needs.

## 2. The Role of Visibility in Campaign Success

Visibility is a key factor in campaign success. The more visible your campaign is in the community, the more likely voters are to recognize your candidate, understand their platform, and consider them a viable option on Election Day.

Importance of Visibility:

- **Name Recognition:** Voters are more likely to support candidates whose names they recognize. Consistent visibility in the community helps build name recognition and familiarity, which can be critical in close races.

- **Perceived Accessibility**: A visible candidate is often perceived as more accessible and in touch with the community's needs. Voters want to support candidates who they believe are listening to them and will represent their interests.

- **Trust and Credibility:** Visibility also builds trust and credibility. When voters see your candidate and campaign actively engaged in the community, it reinforces the idea that they are committed to serving the community's interests.

## 3. Strategies for Increasing Visibility

Increasing visibility in the community requires a combination of strategic planning, consistent effort, and creative outreach.

Strategies for Increasing Visibility:

- **Attend Local Events Regularly:** Make sure your candidate and campaign team are regularly attending local events, from small community meetings to large public gatherings. The more visible your campaign is, the more likely voters are to remember your candidate when it's time to vote.

- **Utilize Campaign Signage:** Use campaign signs, banners, and other visual materials to increase your campaign's visibility. Place signs in high-traffic areas, distribute them to supporters, and ensure that they are prominently displayed at events.

- **Engage with Local Media:** Build relationships with local media outlets and journalists. Secure coverage for your events, participate in interviews, and contribute op-eds or letters to the editor to increase your campaign's visibility in local news.

- **Leverage Social Media:** Use social media to amplify your campaign's visibility online. Regularly post updates, engage with followers, and share content that highlights your candidate's presence in the community. Encourage supporters to share your content to expand your reach.

- **Host High-Visibility Events:** Organize events that attract attention and draw large crowds, such as rallies, debates, or community service projects. These events can generate media coverage, word-of-mouth buzz, and increased visibility for your campaign.

## The Power of Community Engagement

Maximizing your impact as a canvasser goes beyond just knocking on doors—it involves integrating your efforts with community events, coordinating with other campaign strategies, and maintaining a strong, visible presence in the community. By doing so, you can build deeper connections with voters, reinforce your campaign's message across multiple channels, and create a lasting impact that drives success on Election Day.

Community engagement is at the heart of grassroots campaigning. When you actively participate in the life of the community, listen to its members, and respond to their needs, you help build a campaign that truly represents the people it seeks to serve. As you continue your efforts, remember that every event, every conversation, and every interaction is an opportunity to strengthen your campaign's connection with the community and move closer to achieving your goals.

By integrating doorknocking with community events, coordinating with other campaign efforts, and prioritizing visibility and presence, you can maximize your impact and contribute significantly to the success of your campaign. Keep these strategies in mind as you plan your outreach, and remember that the relationships you build in the community are the foundation of a successful campaign.

# Chapter 14: Learning from Each Experience

In any political campaign, each doorknocking experience is an opportunity to learn and improve. The process of reflecting on your interactions with voters, analyzing what worked and what didn't, and sharing insights with your campaign team is crucial for personal growth and the overall success of the campaign.

**How to Debrief and Learn from Your Doorknocking Experiences**

Debriefing after each canvassing session is a critical step in the learning process. It allows you to reflect on your experiences, identify key takeaways, and make adjustments for future interactions. A structured debriefing process can help you gain valuable insights, improve your techniques, and ensure that your efforts are aligned with the campaign's goals.

## 1. The Importance of Debriefing

Debriefing is more than just a review of what happened; it's an essential part of the learning cycle that enables you to grow as a canvasser and contribute more effectively to the campaign. It involves reflecting on your actions, analyzing outcomes, and identifying areas for improvement.

**Why Debriefing Matters:**

- **Promotes Continuous Improvement:** Regular debriefing helps you identify patterns in your interactions, recognize areas where you can improve, and refine your approach over time.

- **Enhances Team Collaboration:** Debriefing with other team members fosters collaboration and knowledge sharing, allowing everyone to learn from each other's experiences.

- **Builds Confidence:** Reflecting on successful interactions and understanding why they worked can boost your confidence and reinforce positive behaviors.

- **Ensures Alignment with Campaign Goals:** Debriefing helps ensure that your canvassing efforts are aligned with the broader campaign strategy, allowing for adjustments when necessary.

## 2. Conducting a Personal Debrief

After each doorknocking session, take some time to conduct a personal debrief. This can be done alone or with a small group of fellow canvassers. The goal is to reflect on your experiences, identify what went well, and consider areas for improvement.

Steps for a Personal Debrief:

- **Find a Quiet Space:** After your canvassing session, find a quiet space where you can reflect without distractions. This could be at home, in your car, or at the campaign office.

- **Review Your Notes:** If you took notes during your canvassing session, review them to refresh your memory of the key interactions. Pay attention to details such as voter concerns, responses, and any follow-up actions needed.

- **Ask Reflective Questions:** Consider the following questions as you debrief:

- What went well during this session? Why do you think it was successful?

- Were there any challenges or difficult interactions? How did you handle them?

- Did you encounter any unexpected situations? How did you adapt?

- Were there any common themes or concerns among the voters you spoke to?

- How did voters respond to your messaging? Were there any messages that resonated particularly well or fell flat?

- **Identify Key Takeaways:** Based on your reflections, identify 2-3 key takeaways that you can apply to future canvassing efforts. These could be specific techniques, adjustments to your approach, or insights into voter behavior.

- **Set Goals for Improvement:** Use your key takeaways to set specific, actionable goals for your next canvassing session. For example, if you noticed that voters were particularly concerned about healthcare, you might focus on refining your talking points on that issue.

## 3. Debriefing with Your Team

Debriefing with your team is an opportunity to share experiences, exchange insights, and collectively analyze the effectiveness of your canvassing efforts. Team debriefs can be formal or informal, depending on the size of the team and the complexity of the campaign.

How to Conduct a Team Debrief:

- **Schedule Regular Debriefs:** Schedule regular debrief sessions with your team, ideally after each canvassing session or at the end of each day. These sessions can be held in person, over the phone, or via video conferencing.

- **Create a Safe Space:** Ensure that the debriefing environment is supportive and non-judgmental. Team members should feel comfortable sharing their experiences, both positive and negative, without fear of criticism.

- **Use a Structured Format:** Follow a structured format to keep the debrief focused and productive. A common format includes:

- **What went well?:** Start by discussing the successes of the session. What worked particularly well, and why?

- **What were the challenges?:** Identify any challenges or obstacles encountered during the session. How were they handled, and what could be done differently next time?

- **What can we improve?:** Brainstorm ways to improve future canvassing efforts. This could involve refining messaging, adjusting routes, or trying new techniques.

- **Next steps:** Identify any follow-up actions that need to be taken, such as contacting specific voters, adjusting the canvassing strategy, or addressing logistical issues.

- **Document Insights:** Assign someone to document the key insights and action items from the debrief session. This ensures that valuable information is captured and can be referenced later.

## 4. The Role of Feedback in Debriefing

Feedback is a crucial component of the debriefing process. It allows you to receive input from others, gain new perspectives, and identify areas for growth. Effective feedback should be specific, constructive, and focused on behavior rather than personality.

Giving and Receiving Feedback:

- **Be Specific:** When giving feedback, be as specific as possible. Instead of saying, "You did a great job," try, "I noticed that you were really effective at addressing voters' concerns about healthcare. Your ability to explain the candidate's policy in a relatable way was impressive."

- **Focus on Behavior:** Frame your feedback around specific behaviors or actions, rather than making general statements about a person. For example, "I noticed that you tended to interrupt voters when they were speaking. Perhaps you could focus more on active listening to ensure that you're fully addressing their concerns."

- **Be Constructive:** Constructive feedback is aimed at helping the recipient improve. Even when pointing out areas for improvement, do so in a way that is supportive and encouraging. For example, "I think you could improve your confidence when talking about economic issues. Maybe we can practice those talking points together before the next session."

- **Seek Feedback from Others:** Actively seek feedback from your team members and supervisors. Ask them what they observed during your canvassing sessions and what suggestions they have for improvement.

## Analyzing What Worked and What Didn't: Adjusting Your Approach

One of the most valuable aspects of debriefing is the opportunity to analyze your canvassing efforts and make adjustments to your approach. By identifying what worked and what didn't, you can continuously refine your techniques and become a more effective canvasser.

## 1. Identifying Successes

Start by identifying the successes of your canvassing session. This involves recognizing the strategies and techniques that were most effective in engaging voters, conveying your message, and securing support for your candidate.

Questions to Identify Successes:

- **Which interactions were the most positive?:** Reflect on the interactions that went particularly well. What made these interactions successful? Was it the way you presented your message, the voter's openness, or something else?

- **What messages resonated with voters?:** Consider which of your talking points or messages seemed to resonate most with voters. Were there specific issues or phrases that elicited strong positive responses?

- **Did you achieve your goals?:** Assess whether you achieved the goals you set before the canvassing session. If your goal was to persuade undecided voters, did you manage to do so? If you aimed to raise awareness about a particular issue, were voters receptive?

- **Were there any unexpected wins?:** Sometimes, success comes in unexpected forms. Perhaps a voter who seemed uninterested at first ended up being highly engaged, or you found a new way to connect with voters that you hadn't tried before.

## 2. Analyzing Challenges and Obstacles

Next, analyze the challenges and obstacles you encountered during your canvassing session. Understanding what didn't work as well as you hoped is key to making improvements in the future.

Questions to Analyze Challenges:

- **What interactions were difficult?:** Reflect on the interactions that were challenging or didn't go as planned. What made these interactions difficult? Was it the voter's attitude, the complexity of the issue, or something else?

- **Did you encounter resistance?:** Consider whether you encountered resistance from voters, and if so, how you responded. Were there specific issues or arguments that voters pushed back on? How could you address these concerns more effectively in the future?

- **Were there any logistical issues?:** Think about any logistical challenges you faced, such as difficulties with your route, problems with materials, or timing issues. How could these be addressed or avoided in future canvassing sessions?

- **What would you do differently?:** Based on your reflections, identify what you would do differently next time. This could involve changing your approach, refining your message, or preparing more thoroughly.

## 3. Adjusting Your Approach

Once you've analyzed your successes and challenges, it's time to adjust your approach. This involves making specific, actionable changes to your canvassing strategy to improve your effectiveness in future sessions.

Strategies for Adjusting Your Approach:

- **Refine Your Messaging:** If certain messages resonated more with voters, consider refining your talking points to emphasize these areas. Conversely, if certain messages fell flat, think about how you can reframe them or focus on different issues.

- **Practice Difficult Conversations:** If you struggled with certain types of conversations, such as handling objections or discussing complex issues, take the time to practice these scenarios. Role-playing with a fellow canvasser or team member can help you build confidence and improve your skills.

- **Adjust Your Route or Timing:** If you encountered logistical issues, such as finding voters not at home or running out of time, consider adjusting your route or timing. You might need to start canvassing earlier, focus on different neighborhoods, or plan more breaks.

- **Enhance Your Listening Skills:** If you found that voters were not as receptive as you hoped, consider focusing on your listening skills. Active listening—showing genuine interest in what the voter is saying, asking follow-up questions, and reflecting back what you've heard—can help build rapport and make voters more open to your message.

- **Seek Additional Training:** If you identified specific areas where you need to improve, seek additional training or resources. This could involve attending a workshop, studying campaign materials, or asking for feedback from more experienced canvassers.

## Sharing Your Insights and Experiences with the Campaign Team

Your experiences in the field are a valuable resource for the entire campaign. Sharing your insights with the campaign team helps ensure that everyone is learning from each other's experiences and that the campaign as a whole is continuously improving.

### 1. The Value of Knowledge Sharing

Sharing your insights and experiences with the campaign team contributes to a culture of continuous learning and improvement. It ensures that valuable information is not siloed and that the entire team can benefit from the lessons learned in the field.

Benefits of Knowledge Sharing:

- **Collective Learning:** When team members share their experiences, everyone benefits from the collective knowledge. This can lead to faster improvements and more effective strategies across the campaign.

- **Avoiding Common Pitfalls:** By sharing challenges and obstacles, you help others avoid making the same mistakes. This can save time and resources and lead to better outcomes in future canvassing efforts.

- **Building Team Cohesion:** Knowledge sharing fosters a sense of collaboration and teamwork. When everyone is contributing to the campaign's success, it builds a stronger, more cohesive team.

## 2. Methods for Sharing Insights

There are several ways to share your insights and experiences with the campaign team, depending on the size of the team, the structure of the campaign, and the resources available.

Ways to Share Insights:

- **Team Meetings:** Regular team meetings are an ideal forum for sharing insights. Each team member can take a few minutes to discuss their experiences, highlight successes, and suggest improvements. These meetings can be held in person, via conference call, or over video chat.

- **Written Reports:** If you prefer to document your experiences in writing, consider creating a brief report or memo after each canvassing session. This can be shared with the campaign leadership or distributed to the team via email or a shared drive.

- **Digital Platforms:** Use digital platforms like Slack, Trello, or Google Docs to share insights and updates with the team in real time. These platforms allow for ongoing communication and make it easy to reference past discussions or documents.

- **One-on-One Conversations:** If you have specific insights that might be particularly valuable to a colleague, consider having a one-on-one conversation. This can be especially helpful if you've noticed something that directly relates to their work or if you want to provide more personalized feedback.

## 3. Encouraging a Culture of Feedback

For knowledge sharing to be effective, it's important to foster a culture of feedback within the campaign team. This means creating an environment where team members feel comfortable sharing their experiences, asking questions, and providing constructive criticism.

Fostering a Feedback Culture:

- **Lead by Example:** Campaign leaders and experienced canvassers should lead by example by openly sharing their own experiences, both successes and challenges. This sets the tone for the rest of the team and encourages others to do the same.

- **Normalize Mistakes:** Normalize the idea that mistakes are a natural part of the learning process. When team members understand that mistakes are opportunities for growth, they're more likely to share their challenges and seek feedback.

- **Provide Structured Opportunities for Feedback:** Create structured opportunities for feedback, such as regular debrief sessions, peer reviews, or feedback forms. These opportunities should be a regular part of the campaign's operations.

- **Celebrate Learning:** Celebrate moments of learning and improvement within the team. When someone shares an insightful experience or makes a significant improvement, acknowledge their contribution and use it as a learning moment for the entire team.

## Continuously Improving Your Effectiveness as a Doorknocker

The most successful canvassers are those who are committed to continuous improvement. By regularly reflecting on your experiences, seeking out new learning opportunities, and applying what you've learned in the field, you can become a more effective and impactful advocate for your candidate.

## 1. The Mindset of Continuous Improvement

Continuous improvement is a mindset that involves always looking for ways to grow and develop, both personally and professionally. It's about being open to feedback, willing to try new approaches, and committed to learning from every experience.

Adopting a Continuous Improvement Mindset:

- **Be Curious:** Approach each canvassing session with curiosity. Ask yourself what you can learn from each interaction, and be open to new perspectives and ideas.

- **Embrace Challenges:** View challenges and obstacles as opportunities for growth rather than setbacks. Each challenge you encounter is a chance to learn and improve.

- **Stay Adaptable:** Be willing to adapt your approach based on what you learn. Continuous improvement requires flexibility and the ability to change course when something isn't working.

- **Seek Out New Learning Opportunities**: Actively seek out opportunities to learn and develop your skills. This could involve attending training sessions, reading campaign materials, or practicing new techniques with a colleague.

## 2. Setting Goals for Improvement

Setting specific, measurable goals for improvement is a key part of the continuous improvement process. These goals should be based on your reflections, feedback from others, and the challenges you've encountered in the field.

How to Set Improvement Goals:

- **Identify Areas for Growth:** Based on your debriefs and feedback, identify specific areas where you want to improve.

This could be a particular skill, such as handling objections, or a broader goal, such as increasing voter engagement.

- **Set SMART Goals:** Use the SMART criteria to set goals that are Specific, Measurable, Achievable, Relevant, and Time-bound. For example, instead of setting a vague goal like "improve my canvassing skills," set a specific goal like "increase my success rate in persuading undecided voters by 10% over the next month."

- **Create an Action Plan:** Develop a concrete action plan for achieving your goals. This might involve specific training exercises, practice sessions, or changes to your canvassing strategy.

- **Monitor Progress:** Regularly monitor your progress toward your goals. Keep track of your successes and challenges, and adjust your action plan as needed.

## 3. Leveraging Training and Resources

To continuously improve as a doorknocker, it's important to take advantage of the training and resources available to you. These tools can provide valuable knowledge, skills, and strategies to enhance your effectiveness in the field.

Utilizing Training and Resources:

- **Attend Training Sessions:** Participate in any training sessions offered by your campaign. These sessions are often designed to address common challenges and provide you with the tools you need to succeed.

- **Study Campaign Materials:** Familiarize yourself with all the campaign materials available, including policy papers, talking points, and voter data. The more you know about your candidate's platform and the issues at stake, the more persuasive you'll be in your conversations with voters.

- **Practice with Peers:** Practice your canvassing skills with fellow team members. Role-playing difficult conversations, refining your messaging, and receiving feedback can help you build confidence and improve your performance.

- **Seek Out External Resources:** Don't limit yourself to the resources provided by the campaign. There are many external resources, such as books, online courses, and webinars, that can help you develop your canvassing skills and deepen your understanding of grassroots campaigning.

## 4. Tracking Your Progress Over Time

To ensure that you're continuously improving, it's important to track your progress over time. This allows you to see how far you've come, identify areas where you still need to grow, and celebrate your successes.

How to Track Your Progress:

- **Keep a Canvassing Journal:** Consider keeping a canvassing journal where you record your experiences, reflections, and progress toward your goals. This journal can serve as a valuable tool for tracking your development and identifying patterns over time.

- **Use Data to Measure Success:** If your campaign uses a CRM system or other data-tracking tools, use this data to measure your success in the field. Track metrics such as the number of voters you've persuaded, the success rate of your follow-up efforts, and the overall effectiveness of your canvassing sessions.

- **Review Your Goals Regularly:** Regularly review the goals you've set for improvement and assess your progress. If you've achieved a goal, set a new one. If you're struggling to make progress, consider adjusting your action plan or seeking additional support.

- **Celebrate Milestones:** As you achieve your goals and milestones, take the time to celebrate your successes. Recognizing your achievements helps reinforce positive behaviors and motivates you to continue improving.

## The Journey of Continuous Learning

Learning from each doorknocking experience is an ongoing journey that requires reflection, analysis, and a commitment to continuous improvement. By debriefing after each session, analyzing what worked and what didn't, sharing your insights with the campaign team, and setting goals for improvement, you can become a more effective and impactful canvasser.

Remember that every interaction with a voter is an opportunity to learn and grow. Whether you encounter success or face challenges, each experience adds to your knowledge and skills, helping you become a stronger advocate for your candidate and a more effective member of your campaign team.

As you continue your canvassing efforts, keep the principles of continuous learning at the forefront of your approach. By doing so, you'll not only improve your own effectiveness but also contribute to the overall success of the campaign. Stay curious, embrace challenges, and always be open to learning from each experience—this mindset will serve you well, not just in your current campaign but in all future endeavors.

# Chapter 15: Staying Motivated and Energized

Political campaigns, particularly those that rely heavily on grassroots efforts like doorknocking, are marathons, not sprints. The physical and emotional demands of canvassing can take a toll on even the most passionate and dedicated campaigners. As the campaign progresses, maintaining enthusiasm and energy becomes increasingly challenging, yet it is crucial for sustaining the momentum needed to achieve victory.

## Maintaining Enthusiasm Over the Course of a Long Campaign

Campaigning is often grueling work, requiring long hours, frequent rejection, and the persistence to keep going despite setbacks. Maintaining enthusiasm over the course of a long campaign requires intentional effort and a strategic approach to self-care, motivation, and resilience.

## 1. Understanding the Challenges of Sustained Campaigning

To maintain your motivation throughout a campaign, it's important to understand the common challenges you'll face and how they can impact your enthusiasm. By anticipating these challenges, you can develop strategies to overcome them and keep your energy levels high.

Common Challenges in Long Campaigns:

- **Physical Exhaustion:** Canvassing often involves walking long distances, carrying materials, and spending extended periods outdoors, sometimes in challenging weather conditions. Over time, this physical exertion can lead to exhaustion, making it harder to stay motivated.

- **Emotional Fatigue:** Repeatedly facing rejection, encountering hostile or indifferent voters, and dealing with the uncertainty of the campaign's outcome can contribute to emotional fatigue. This can diminish your enthusiasm and make it difficult to stay positive.

- **Monotony and Burnout:** The repetitive nature of canvassing—knocking on doors, delivering the same messages, and following similar routines day after day—can lead to feelings of monotony and burnout. Without variety and breaks, even the most committed campaigners can lose their spark.

- **Discouragement from Setbacks:** Setbacks are inevitable in any campaign, whether it's losing key volunteers, facing unexpected opposition, or seeing poll numbers that don't reflect your efforts. These setbacks can be discouraging and may cause doubts about the effectiveness of your work.

## 2. Strategies for Maintaining Motivation

Maintaining motivation during a long campaign requires a combination of self-care, goal-setting, and finding ways to renew your enthusiasm regularly. The following strategies can help you stay energized and committed, even when the going gets tough.

Prioritize Self-Care:

- **Physical Self-Care:** Take care of your body by getting enough sleep, eating nutritious meals, and staying hydrated. Regular exercise can also help maintain your energy levels and reduce stress. Make sure to listen to your body and take breaks when needed to avoid burnout.

- **Mental and Emotional Self-Care:** Mental and emotional well-being are just as important as physical health. Practice mindfulness techniques, such as meditation or deep breathing, to manage stress. Engage in activities that bring you joy and relaxation outside of campaign work, such as hobbies, spending time with loved ones, or simply taking time for yourself.

- **Avoid Overworking:** It's easy to fall into the trap of overworking during a campaign, but this can quickly lead to burnout. Set boundaries for yourself, such as designated days off or specific hours when you step away from campaign work. Remember, pacing yourself is crucial for maintaining long-term motivation.

Set Clear, Achievable Goals:

- **Short-Term Goals:** Break down the campaign into smaller, manageable tasks by setting short-term goals. These goals should be specific, measurable, and achievable within a short time frame, such as a day or a week. For example, set a goal to reach a certain number of voters each day or to secure a specific number of commitments for support.

- **Celebrate Small Wins:** Celebrating small victories along the way can provide a sense of accomplishment and boost your morale. Whether it's successfully persuading an undecided voter, finishing a challenging day of canvassing, or receiving positive feedback from a voter, take time to acknowledge and celebrate these achievements.

- **Stay Focused on the Bigger Picture:** While short-term goals are important, it's equally crucial to keep the bigger picture in mind. Remind yourself of the overall mission and why you're involved in the campaign. Visualize the impact your efforts will have on election day and beyond.

Find Inspiration in Others:

- **Share Stories with Fellow Canvassers:** One of the most powerful ways to stay motivated is by connecting with your fellow campaigners. Share your successes, challenges, and experiences with others who are on the same journey. Hearing about their victories and challenges can reignite your passion and remind you that you're part of a larger movement.

- **Learn from Past Campaigns:** Look to successful past campaigns for inspiration. Study how other campaigners overcame obstacles, stayed motivated, and ultimately achieved their goals. Learning from their experiences can provide valuable insights and remind you that persistence pays off.

Create Variety in Your Routine:

- **Mix Up Your Canvassing Locations:** If possible, rotate the neighborhoods or areas where you canvass to add variety to your routine. A change of scenery can prevent monotony and keep your work feeling fresh.

- **Alternate Campaign Activities:** In addition to doorknocking, consider participating in other campaign activities, such as phone banking, event organizing, or social media outreach. Switching between different tasks can help maintain your enthusiasm and prevent burnout.

- **Take on New Challenges:** Challenge yourself by taking on new roles or responsibilities within the campaign. Whether it's training new volunteers, leading a canvassing team, or organizing a local event, stepping outside your comfort zone can reinvigorate your passion for the campaign.

**Inspirational Stories from Successful Doorknockers**

Hearing stories of successful doorknockers who have faced challenges similar to yours can be a powerful source of motivation. These stories illustrate the impact that grassroots campaigning can have and serve as reminders that your efforts are making a difference.

**1. Overcoming Rejection: The Story of Emily, the Reluctant Canvasser**

Emily was a first-time canvasser who joined a local campaign because she was passionate about the issues the candidate stood for. However, she was hesitant about knocking on doors due to her fear of rejection. In her first week, Emily faced numerous closed doors, dismissive comments, and voters who simply weren't interested in talking. She began to doubt whether she was cut out for canvassing.

But instead of giving up, Emily sought advice from more experienced canvassers. They encouraged her to focus on the positive interactions she had, no matter how small, and to see each rejection as a step closer to finding a voter who would be receptive. Emily adjusted her mindset and adopted a more resilient attitude.

As she continued canvassing, Emily started to notice small victories—a voter who initially seemed disinterested but ended up asking thoughtful questions, a young person who was inspired by the candidate's stance on climate change, and a family that committed to voting because of her visit. By the end of the campaign, Emily had become one of the most effective canvassers on her team, and she realized that overcoming rejection had made her stronger and more determined.

**Lesson:** Rejection is an inevitable part of canvassing, but it doesn't define your success. Every "no" brings you closer to a "yes." Embrace rejection as part of the process and focus on the positive impact you're making, one voter at a time.

## 2. Making a Difference: The Story of Carlos, the Community Connector

Carlos was a seasoned canvasser who had participated in multiple campaigns over the years. In one particularly challenging campaign, Carlos was assigned to canvass in a neighborhood that had been historically neglected by political candidates. The residents were skeptical and mistrustful of anyone associated with politics.

Instead of being discouraged, Carlos saw this as an opportunity to build trust and make a meaningful connection with the community. He spent extra time listening to residents, asking about their concerns, and learning about the issues that mattered most to them. Carlos didn't just talk about the candidate's platform—he made it personal, showing how the candidate's policies would directly benefit the community.

Over time, Carlos became a familiar face in the neighborhood. He attended local events, helped organize community meetings, and even volunteered for local causes unrelated to the campaign. His genuine commitment to the community earned him the respect and trust of the residents.

On election day, Carlos saw the results of his efforts. The neighborhood, which had previously shown low voter turnout, had one of the highest turnouts in the district. Many residents told Carlos that they voted because they felt heard and valued for the first time.

**Lesson:** Building trust and making personal connections with voters can have a profound impact on a campaign. When you invest in the community and show that you care about the issues that matter to them, you can inspire people to take action and participate in the political process.

### 3. Turning a Campaign Around: The Story of Sarah, the Relentless Advocate

Sarah joined a campaign that was struggling to gain traction. The candidate was well-meaning and passionate, but the campaign lacked organization and momentum. Voter engagement was low, and morale among volunteers was dwindling.

Instead of accepting the situation, Sarah decided to take action. She started by reorganizing the canvassing efforts, creating clear goals and schedules for volunteers. She held regular training sessions to equip volunteers with the skills they needed to be effective canvassers. Sarah also focused on improving communication within the team, ensuring that everyone felt supported and informed.

Sarah's relentless efforts began to pay off. Volunteers became more motivated and confident, voter engagement increased, and the campaign started to gain momentum. Sarah's leadership and dedication inspired others to step up and contribute in new ways.

By the end of the campaign, the candidate had gained significant support, and the once-struggling campaign had turned into a competitive race. Although the candidate didn't win, they performed far better than anyone had anticipated, thanks in large part to Sarah's determination and hard work.

**Lesson:** One person's dedication can make a significant difference in a campaign's success. By taking initiative, organizing effectively, and inspiring others, you can turn around even the most challenging situations and make a lasting impact.

## The Long-Term Benefits of Grassroots Political Involvement

While the immediate goal of canvassing is to win an election, the long-term benefits of grassroots political involvement extend far beyond a single campaign. By participating in grassroots efforts, you not only contribute to the democratic process but also develop valuable skills, build lasting relationships, and become a more informed and engaged citizen.

### 1. Developing Valuable Skills

Grassroots political involvement offers a unique opportunity to develop a wide range of skills that are applicable in both personal and professional contexts.

Skills Gained Through Canvassing:

- **Communication Skills:** Canvassing hones your ability to communicate effectively with people from diverse backgrounds. You learn to articulate complex ideas clearly, listen actively, and engage in meaningful dialogue.

- **Persuasion and Negotiation:** Canvassing often involves persuading undecided voters or addressing objections. This helps you develop skills in persuasion and negotiation, which are valuable in many areas of life.

- **Leadership and Teamwork:** Participating in a campaign requires working collaboratively with others, often in high-pressure situations. You develop leadership skills by organizing efforts, motivating volunteers, and managing tasks.

- **Problem-Solving and Adaptability:** Campaigns are dynamic and unpredictable, requiring you to think on your feet and adapt to changing circumstances. You learn to solve problems quickly and effectively, a skill that is highly valued in any profession.

## 2. Building Lasting Relationships

Grassroots campaigning brings together people who share a common goal, creating a sense of camaraderie and community. The relationships you build during a campaign can have lasting benefits, both personally and professionally.

The Value of Relationships Built During Campaigns:

- **Networking Opportunities:** Campaigns provide an excellent opportunity to network with like-minded individuals, including fellow volunteers, campaign staff, community leaders, and even elected officials. These connections can lead to future opportunities in politics, advocacy, or other fields.

- **Lifelong Friendships:** The shared experience of working on a campaign can forge strong bonds and lifelong friendships. Many campaigners find that the relationships they build during a campaign continue long after the election is over.

- **Community Engagement:** Grassroots campaigning often brings you into contact with community members and organizations that you might not have otherwise engaged with. This increased involvement in your community can lead to a deeper understanding of local issues and a greater sense of belonging.

## 3. Becoming a More Informed and Engaged Citizen

One of the most significant long-term benefits of grassroots political involvement is the opportunity to become a more informed and engaged citizen. By participating in a campaign, you gain a deeper understanding of the political process, the issues at stake, and the impact of your vote.

Benefits of Being an Informed and Engaged Citizen:

- **Increased Political Awareness:** Campaigning requires you to stay informed about current events, policy issues, and the positions of various candidates. This increased political awareness can help you make more informed decisions as a voter and advocate for the issues that matter to you.

- **Empowerment and Advocacy:** Grassroots involvement empowers you to take an active role in shaping the future of your community and country. You learn how to advocate effectively for your beliefs and how to mobilize others to do the same.

- **Civic Responsibility:** By participating in the democratic process, you fulfill an important civic responsibility. Your involvement helps ensure that the voices of ordinary citizens are heard and that the government remains accountable to the people it serves.

## Preparing for Election Day and Celebrating Your Contributions

As the campaign reaches its final stages, it's essential to stay focused and motivated to ensure a strong finish. Preparing for election day and celebrating your contributions afterward are key to maintaining your energy and enthusiasm.

## 1. Preparing for the Final Push

The final days leading up to election day are often the most intense and demanding part of the campaign. Staying organized, focused, and motivated during this time is crucial for achieving the best possible outcome.

Strategies for the Final Push:

- **Intensify Your Efforts:** In the days leading up to election day, intensify your canvassing efforts to reach as many voters as possible. This may involve longer hours, more frequent follow-ups, and increased outreach through phone banking, mailers, and digital campaigns.

- **Focus on GOTV (Get Out the Vote):** The final days of the campaign are all about GOTV efforts. Focus on mobilizing your supporters, ensuring that they know where and how to vote, and reminding them of the importance of their participation.

- **Stay Organized:** Organization is key to a successful final push. Make sure that all volunteers are clear on their roles and responsibilities, that materials are prepared and distributed efficiently, and that communication channels are open and effective.

- **Take Care of Yourself:** While the final days of a campaign are demanding, it's important not to neglect self-care. Make sure to get enough rest, eat well, and manage stress to ensure that you're in the best possible shape for election day.

## 2. Election Day: Putting It All Together

Election day is the culmination of all your hard work. It's a day of intense activity, where every effort is focused on getting supporters to the polls and ensuring a smooth voting process.

Key Election Day Activities:

- **Last-Minute Canvassing:** Continue canvassing on election day to remind voters to get to the polls. Focus on those who may need an extra nudge, such as undecided voters or those who have expressed support but haven't yet voted.

- **Transportation and Assistance:** Offer transportation or assistance to voters who may have difficulty getting to the polls. This could include organizing rides, providing information on polling locations, or helping with absentee or early voting.

- **Monitor Polls and Voter Turnout:** Work with the campaign team to monitor voter turnout and ensure that supporters are showing up to vote. Be prepared to respond quickly to any issues that arise, such as long lines, confusion about polling places, or misinformation.

- **Celebrate Your Efforts:** Throughout the day, take moments to reflect on the hard work you've put into the campaign. Acknowledge the contributions of your fellow canvassers and volunteers, and keep the atmosphere positive and encouraging.

## 3. Celebrating Your Contributions

Regardless of the election's outcome, it's important to celebrate your contributions and recognize the impact of your efforts. Campaigning is hard work, and taking time to acknowledge and celebrate what you've achieved is essential for maintaining morale and motivation for future endeavors.

Ways to Celebrate Your Contributions:

- **Post-Election Gathering:** Organize a post-election gathering with your fellow campaigners to celebrate your hard work. Whether it's a formal event or an informal get-together, this is an opportunity to share stories, express gratitude, and enjoy the camaraderie of the team.

- **Reflect on Your Achievements:** Take time to reflect on the skills you've developed, the relationships you've built, and the impact you've made during the campaign. Write down your thoughts or share them with others to create a lasting record of your experience.

- **Acknowledge the Campaign's Impact:** Even if your candidate didn't win, remember that your efforts contributed to raising awareness about important issues, mobilizing voters, and strengthening the democratic process. Celebrate the broader impact of the campaign, not just the outcome.

- **Look Forward to Future Involvement:** Use the momentum and experience gained from the campaign to plan for future political involvement. Whether it's participating in another campaign, advocating for specific issues, or staying active in your community, recognize that your contributions have laid the foundation for ongoing engagement.

Staying motivated and energized throughout a long political campaign is a challenge, but it's also an incredibly rewarding experience. By prioritizing self-care, setting clear goals, finding inspiration in the stories of others, and recognizing the long-term benefits of grassroots involvement, you can maintain your enthusiasm and make a lasting impact.

As you prepare for election day and reflect on your contributions, remember that the work you've done is meaningful and significant. Celebrate your achievements, both big and small, and take pride in the role you've played in the democratic process. Whether your candidate wins or loses, your efforts have contributed to something greater—building a more engaged, informed, and active citizenry.

As you move forward, carry the lessons you've learned and the relationships you've built with you. Grassroots campaigning is not just about a single election; it's about fostering a culture of participation and empowerment that will continue to shape the future. Stay motivated, stay involved, and continue to make a difference in your community and beyond.

# Don't miss out!

Visit the website below and you can sign up to receive emails whenever Bradley Hall publishes a new book. There's no charge and no obligation.

https://books2read.com/r/B-A-SCSZ-RHAZE

**BOOKS 2 READ**

Connecting independent readers to independent writers.

# Also by Bradley Hall

The Enneagram and Money
Why Won't My Children Talk to Me? A Book For
Conservatives
Embracing Complexity
Embracing the Turbo Dude Lifestyle
The 13 Days of Christmas
Enneapolitics
Knocking on Democracy's Door